The Nature of Mammals

Scientific consultants to the series: WALTER TOVELL, PhD, Director, Royal Ontario Museum; J. MURRAY SPEIRS, PhD, Department of Zoology, University of Toronto

ISBN: 0-9196-4411-2

Natural Science of Canada Limited
58 Northline Road, Toronto, Ontario M4B 3E5

Publisher: Jack McClelland
Managing Director: William Belt
Editors: Stanley Fillmore/Jennifer Glossop
Assistant Editors: Kathy Vanderlinden/Betty Kennedy

Page 1: A badger at his burrow
Page 2: Big-horned sheep in Alberta
Page 4: White-tailed deer fawn
Page 6: Bison grazing

CONTENTS

INTRODUCTION

Mammals have always fascinated man the mammal. They were the subject of cave drawings by primitive men and in ancient times were kept in menageries, a practice that has its modern counterpart in zoos, still dominated by mammals. Through the ages they have been our principal domestic animals. Indeed, the word 'animal' is often used as if it meant 'mammal.'

Our interest in mammals is no idle curiosity, for they have provided men with food, clothing, shelter, help in the chase, protection, labour, and transportation, as well as companionship. They have profoundly affected the development of civilizations and influenced history by spreading diseases such as plague. In Canada, not only have native peoples depended on fur-bearers, but European exploration followed routes established by the fur trade. It is no accident that the beaver should be a national emblem, for trade in beaver pelts affected the early settlement and economy of the country. Even today, fur trading, hunting, and tourism depend on wild mammals and, like animal husbandry, are substantial industries. However, many species, such as buffalo and whales, that were once important are now sadly depleted.

Our attitude to other mammals reflects a man-centred view of the universe deeply ingrained in our culture. We tend to evaluate animals by their direct usefulness to us. Later in the book we shall see that this attitude endangers them and, in the long run, us as well. The best antidote I know to a narrow view of nature is to become familiar with wild animals. The more we understand them, the more we respect and value all of nature and see ourselves in a different light.

This book introduces us to the lives of mammals in a Canadian setting. It presents the findings of naturalists and scientists for the general reader. But to read about animals is only a beginning. I hope the reader will be stimulated to seek out wild mammals for himself.

Mammals are very diverse. They range in size from the tiny shrews to the giant whales in our coastal waters. Different mammals fly, climb trees, run on the ground, and burrow in the soil. They occupy nearly every habitat from the high Arctic to the fields and forests of southern Canada. Some are rare but meadow mice may number more than one hundred to the acre. Even in cities, raccoons, skunks, foxes, woodchuck, squirrels, and a host of smaller species hold their own.

WAYLAND DREW   DON BALDWIN   RUSSELL RUTTER   ROBERT COLLINS

Despite their fascination, far less amateur study has been devoted to mammals than to birds. There are fewer kinds of mammals – about 200 in Canada compared with over 500 birds. However, I think the reason for their comparative neglect lies in their secretive habits. Many are active only at night and are hidden in trees or burrows by day. Though they are all around us, they are harder to see and hear than birds. But this presents a challenge to the naturalist. At night, mammals can be watched by red light to which they are insensitive or even under white light if undisturbed. I recently watched a skunk digging in my city garden under a spotlight. If mammals cannot always be seen they leave telltale signs of their activities – tracks in snow or mud, burrows and other works, hair, droppings, and food remains. As detectives, we can try to interpret their activities from these clues. A later chapter describes how people make contact with wolves by howling. Much has been learned about smaller mammals by catching them alive in baited traps. Of course, many larger mammals can be observed in parks. On open plains, even smaller rodents can be watched with binoculars. The reader who takes the trouble to study mammals will be amply repaid by the pleasure derived and by the mind-expanding view of the natural world that comes from familiarity with the ways of other species.

J. BRUCE FALLS
University of Toronto

THE AUTHORS

WAYLAND DREW is a free-lance writer and amateur naturalist. His recent work includes a novel, *The Wabeno Feast*, as well as essays on conservation for *Canadian Forum* and *Ontario Naturalist*. DON BALDWIN is presently a biology teacher at Upper Canada College. He is the author of many papers on ornithology and natural history. RUSSELL J. RUTTER has produced *The Raven*, the weekly publication of the Ministry of Natural Resources, for the past fifteen years. He is a former director and honorary member of the Federation of Ontario Naturalists. ROBERT COLLINS has been a working journalist for the last twenty-four years. He is currently a contributing editor of *Reader's Digest* (Canada).

9

PART ONE
WHAT IS A MAMMAL?

Dawn. A wolf's call pierces the frozen air, and the man carrying the gun stops to listen. The man's breath streams from his nostrils, thickening the ice which has encrusted his beard and the fur edge of his parka. Only a small portion of his face is exposed, but the bite of the cold there reminds him that without his clothes he would be dead in moments. Unlike the wolf, he is a stranger in this land. He survives by imitating those animals whose domain he has invaded and whose ancestory has moulded them for life in the stern northern climate. Close to his skin he wears a soft animal material – wool or rabbit's fur – covered by thick outer garments. His hands are swathed in mitts of the same material, leaving only his muscular thumb free of the other fingers. Mukluks cover his feet. Even his snowshoes, woven of animal gut, imitate the spreading pads which support the wolf in deep snow. Because he cannot duplicate the wolf's fangs and claws, or the slashing

The sound of a timber wolf howling is an unforgettable part of the Canadian wilderness. For the early settlers, wolves were a source of considerable concern.

hooves of the moose, he carries a rifle. Exquisitely precise, it and the bullets nestled in its magazine are the products of an evolutionary process which stretches back for at least three million years. No other animal could have made that tool because only man possesses the necessary forethought, the imagination, and the all-important thumb. These features have spread *Homo sapiens* throughout the world and made him, for the moment, the dominant species of mammal.

Again the wolf howls, farther off. The man grunts, shifts his rifle to his left hand, and proceeds in the opposite direction. He has decided not to hunt. The tracks of carnivore and primate diverge in the fresh snow.

Fifteen hundred miles to the south, a farmer opens his door to a crisp morning. He pulls on his cap. For a moment before walking to the barn he stands on his porch and gazes through patches of mist at his domain. He owns this land. The labour of his ancestors won the fields from the forest, and the annual round of his planting and harvesting continues what they began. A dairyman, he and other breeders have so refined one species of domestic ungulate that it is a placid milk-machine, and when he arrives in the barn he will attach automatic equip-

11

ment to the cows' unnaturally pendulous udders. No other animal could have devised that milker, or built the electric plants which feed it energy. Only man could have cleared the fields of this farm and erected the fences which separate pasture from woodlot. For the moment there is no doubt that man is in control – or, at least, that he has radically altered this environment to suit his purposes. But as the farmer begins his walk to the barn he is watched by quick, wild eyes – the shrew's, the rat's, the woodchuck's, the fox's. Unknown to him, an opossum has found his woodlot during the night, and from a low branch this most primitive of Canadian mammals watches him implacably. Her ancestors wandered far during their millions of years on earth, and her adaptability and doggedness have helped her to survive while brighter creatures perished. This winter she may lose the tips of her ears and tail to frost, but in the spring there will be new babies in her pouch, new wanderers to extend the opossum's range.

For at least sixty million years before the arrival of man, other mammals flourished in North America. Most of the species which evolved during that time we shall never see, for they have long since become extinct, victims of environmental changes to which they could not adapt. Only the fossil record remains to tell us that *Eohippus*, a species of horse no larger than a lapdog, once roamed the Canadian prairie, or that rhinoceros-like creatures such as the *Eobasileus*, the *Uintatherium*, and the *Coryphodon* once wallowed in tropical northern swamps. A million years ago, just before the glaciers covered nearly all of Canada, many mammalian species had evolved into familiar forms. Horses and bison shared their ranges. Rodents scampered everywhere, preyed upon by many types of carnivores. With the withdrawal of the ice, the first human hunters crossed over Bering Strait and cautiously headed south. They found a profusion of animal life, including the woolly mammoth, the sabre-toothed tiger, great ground sloths (one as large as an elephant), camels, horses, and lions. Life was risky, but by then man had developed two great skills which other mammals lacked: tools and abstract ideas.

1 MANY VARIETIES

Animals communicate by different types of signals. Colours, gestures and sounds all play their part, but for most mammals scent is vital. Blind polar bears can survive by relying on smell alone. Carnivores can distinguish scores of scent nuances, and for its own protection the fawn lacks any deer odour during its first days of life. To compensate for its loss of smell, the star-nosed mole has grown a fifth paw on its snout, with twenty-two fleshy 'fingers.'

So little is smell valued among men, however, that insurance companies do not even consider its loss a disability. Instead, man's ancestors stressed sight, hearing, and speech. The pronghorn antelope can see better than man (his vision is the equivalent of human sight assisted by eight-power binoculars); whales send complicated messages over great distances; and bats can emit 250 clicking sounds per second, ranging to a frequency of 100,000 cycles per second, far beyond the 16,000 cps upper limit of the human ear. But true speech, with the cultural legacy it makes possible, is uniquely human.

Finding names for the furry, warm-blooded vertebrates with which man shared the earth probably helped language to evolve, and no doubt most primitive men had a name for mammals as a class distinct from fish, reptiles, and birds. Modern scientists who seek to pinpoint similarities and differences between animal species are called taxonomists, and it is they, following the lead of the eighteenth-century classifier, Linnaeus, who are responsible for our system of naming living things. Like other sciences, taxonomy changes with changing knowledge, and unless we are specialists we need not be concerned with whether the odd- and the even-toed ungulates are two separate orders, or whether seals and walruses should be considered apart from other carnivores. Nor need we use the taxonomist's whole hierarchy of categories.

The powerful sabre-toothed tiger had long upper canine teeth, capable of inflicting deep, slashing wounds. It survived on the North American continent until the end of the Pleistocene epoch.

ABOVE: *MOLE*   BELOW: *PORCUPINE*

ABOVE: *BAT*   BELOW: *KILLER WHALE*

BELOW: *WALRUS*

BELOW: *MULE DEER*

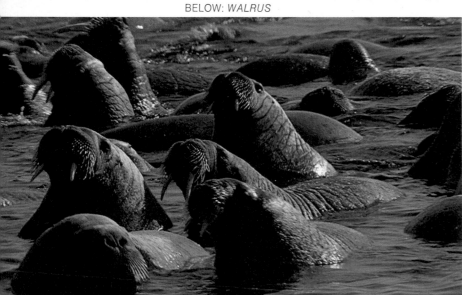

ABOVE: *PIKA*   BELOW: *WOLVERINE*

BELOW: *HORSES*

The *class* Mammalia is composed of several *orders*, each of which is composed of *families* and *species*. Each family usually contains a number of species, and each order a variety of families. All display the characteristics of their class.

Members of nineteen living orders compose the class Mammalia, and many of these may be seen by spending an evening in a city park or ravine. The ravenous little shrew is an Insectivore, consuming his body weight in grubs and insects every day. Although he also eats insects, the bat is distinguished by the elongated finger bones which form the struts of his wing, and bats are thus called Chiroptera, 'hand-wings.' Squirrels and chipmunks are gnawers, Rodentia, the largest and most widespread mammalian order. Because he is shaped like a hare the rabbit is a Lagomorpha. The cats hunting in the underbrush and the dogs trotting at their masters' heels are both carnivores. The policeman's horse is an ungulate, and its rider is a Primate.

If there is a good zoo nearby one may see members of some exotic orders – flying lemurs, aardvarks, armadillos, sloths, hydraxes, and perhaps even a rare pangolin. If the zoo is very commodious it may even have a pair of 'long-noses,' elephants of the order Proboscidea.

An aquarium – and a huge one – would be required to display members of the other mammalian orders – gentle dugongs and manatees; sea-lions and walruses; dolphins, porpoises, and whales. But even at the best zoo in the world you will not see the oldest of living mammals, for the duckbilled platypus will not survive in captivity.

Not all orders of mammals are to be found in Canada. The mole is a member of the order Insectivora. All bats belong to the order Chiroptera. The little pika is a member of the order Lagomorpha as are rabbits. The porcupine, a rodent, belongs to the same order as beavers, rats, and squirrels. The killer whale belongs to one of the two orders of aquatic mammals. The next major order, Carnivora, includes wolverines, wolves, and bears, among others. Seals and walruses are members of the order Pinnipedia. Deer and horses, similar in appearance, belong to separate orders, Artiodactyla and Perissodactyla.

No matter what their differences, all of these creatures share five basic characteristics: First, mammals have hair. Second, the young of all mammals are fed by mammary glands. Third, mammals are warm-blooded (homeothermal) and have four-chambered hearts which separate venous and arterial blood. Fourth, mammals have a diaphragm between their thoracic and abdominal cavities. Finally, the mammalian brain is generally larger than that found in any other class.

Although there are several skeletal peculiarities as well, these five are the principal distinguishing characteristics of mammals. How they came into being, and how they combine with other mutations and adaptations to produce the 5,000 living species is the aspect of evolution which most immediately concerns us.

2 MUTATION AND SELECTION

The tremendous variety of life on earth (a million species of animals and a quarter million kinds of plants) is the product of twin evolutionary processes: mutation and natural selection.

In reproducing itself, a species does more than make perfect carbon copies. It experiments constantly with variations on its basic genetic pattern; nature then 'selects' those individuals who are most fit to breed and to pass on their characteristics. When a pattern is accidently miscopied within a cell, a mutation has occurred. Mutation is a totally random process, usually producing freaks whose chances of breeding are drastically reduced. Occasionally, however, a mutant strain meshes with its environment in such a way that it flourishes, leading to fresh experiments and new varieties of genetic structure. All life on earth is the result of this questing lottery, and all life perpetuates it.

Three hundred and sixty-five million years ago, this process produced a fish whose flippers had strengthened into legs and who had primitive lungs as well as gills. No doubt there were many similar creatures, the results of countlesss experiments over millions of years, and when they began to draw themselves up out of the warm seas and to travel overland from pool to pool, staying in air for longer and longer periods, the first amphibians had begun to evolve. Within the next one hundred million years mutation and natural selection had given some species a new, tough, leathery kind of egg capable of hatching on land, and at that point the evolution and diffusion of reptiles had begun.

This then is the progression of evolution – from invertebrate sea organisms, to vertebrate fish, to amphibians, to reptiles, to birds and mammals. The entire process has occurred over several billion years. Only within the last 200 million years have mammals come on the scene, and for half of that time they remained tiny, furtive creatures dominated by overbearing cousins.

Paradoxically, the most awesome reptiles to have appeared on earth were misnamed because Greek, the favourite language of taxonomists, had no word for reptile. Hence dinosaurs were 'terrible lizards,' although many bore little resemblance to lizards and not all were terrible. Hundreds of species evolved during their long reign on earth. Some glided on huge skin wings. Some returned to the seas, foreshadowing mammalian whales and porpoises. Some, like *Triceratops* or like *Stegosaurus* dragging his plated tail, rumbled like tanks across the land, while the lordly *Brontosaurus* lifted his head above Jurassic swamps. For 135 million years dinosaurs held sway, constantly mutating, constantly adapting, producing forms of marvellous variety and sophistication. Their success speaks for itself.

At that time the earth was a smooth and steamy place. Forests spread up to the poles, the continents lacked the mountain ranges they bear today, and the oceans were probably contoured and shaped much differently. During this time, some varieties of pre-dinosaurian reptiles began to make interesting changes in their structures. For one thing, their teeth became better adapted to cutting and chewing rather than merely to clamping on their prey and gulping it

All mammals share five characteristics: (1) hair, (2) mammary glands, (3) a four-chambered heart and warm blood, (4) a diaphragm, and (5) a larger brain.

Mammalian Characteristics

1

2

3

4

5

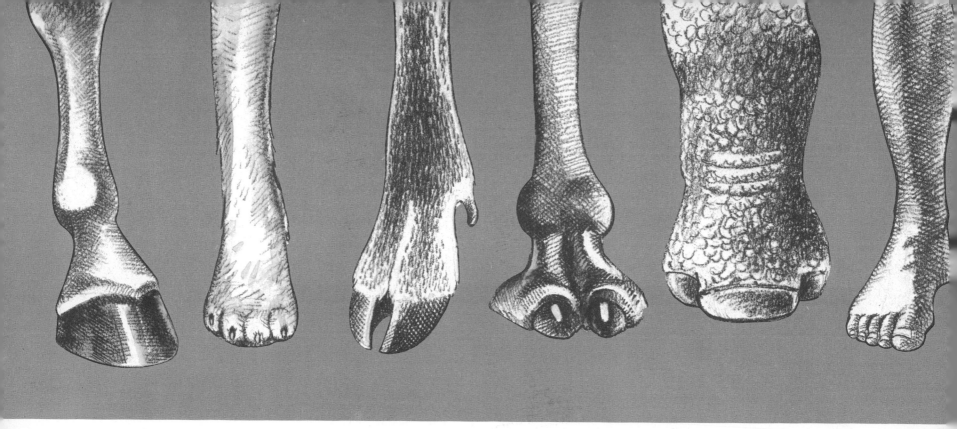

The diversity of these mammalian feet indicates the variety of terrain occupied and contrasting sizes attained by mammals. In the horse and deer, the original toes developed into hoofs. The rhinoceros and camel evolved feet that could support their weight on soft surfaces. The dog, like other carnivores, has well-developed claws. The feet of man differ from those of other primates in that his big toe has shifted forward parallel to his other toes.

down. This change was accompanied by a modification of the lower jaw; the multi-boned reptilian jaw fused and strengthened into the single piece which characterizes mammalian jaws today. Second, their backbones also strengthened, and their legs began to lift their bodies higher off the ground. To give added support, the legs were tucked under the body, with the knees pointing forward and the elbows pointing back, rather than projecting to the sides in the comparatively clumsy manner of reptiles. The result was a creature with more agility and more speed.

Speed is an obvious advantage for any hunting animal, and the longer that speed can be maintained, the greater the advantage. But in order to move fast for long distances, an animal must have a constantly high metabolic rate – that is, it must be capable of quickly converting stored energy and of continuing to do so for sustained periods. Further, it must be able to cool itself in warm weather and to conserve heat in cold. Reptiles are 'cold-blooded'; they have a low metabolism in cold weather and their internal temperature approximates that of their environment. Although this means that they can survive on comparatively little food, it also means that they are restricted in their movements. When the sun grows too hot, they must find shade; when the climate cools, they sink into a heat-conserving torpor.

Obviously, an animal that could evolve the means of controlling its internal temperature regardless of environment would have a distinct advantage. Birds evolved from reptilian ancestors. To this day birds retain many reptilian traits – they lay eggs and their young are equipped with an 'egg tooth'; scales still cover their legs; their shoulder girdle, though hollow and light, is very like a reptile's. The evolution of feathers for flight and insulation, however, was decisive.

3 BEAVERS AND MAD HATTERS

One researcher has counted sixty theories to explain the sudden disappearance of the dinosaurs. Two of the most likely involve extremes of temperature – either the earth grew hot enough to sterilize them by killing their sperm, or else it grew so cold that they fell into a final torpor.

In any case, mammals as well as birds had meantime equipped themselves to deal with extremes of temperature; and when the age of dinosaurs ended about 63 million years ago, the age of mammals began. Mammals quickly diversified to fill vacant ecological niches, adapting to life underground, in the trees and air, in water, and in a variety of terrains. Although some species chose to dispense with their fur at a later date, all had it at first; like the bird's feathers, it was decisive in preserving them, not only when the dinosaurs perished, but also through the ice ages which have since spread over North America. Unlike the dinosaurs, mammals were able to change with changing conditions.

Probably no mammal is more familiar to Canadians than the beaver. His hunched profile adorned the first Canadian stamp and is still carried on the Canadian nickel. Hochelaga, the Indian name by which Champlain knew Montreal, means beaver dam. Our respect for this chunky rodent has a solid historical base, for his pelt was the mainstay of the fur trade, and in the fur trade lay the beginnings of the Canadian nation.

Of course, men had hunted the beaver long before Champlain's arrival. The first North Americans found beavers as large as small bears. The beaver was unlikely to have been a stranger to these hunters in the new world, for European beaver fossils have been found which date back 60 million years, and man had probably long relied on beaver skins for clothing.

In the early 1700s, however, a new interest was aroused in beaver fur. Fashionable Europeans demanded felt hats, and the soft, small, inner hairs of beaver fur made the most luxurious felt of all. Because the process of felt-making involved large amounts of mercury, many hatters were literally mad, their brains addled by mercury poisoning. Hat styles

19

varied – tall, squat, broad, and drooping – but for several decades the demand for beaver fur remained strong, and those decades were the most eventful in Canadian exploration. From Montreal and the east coast of Hudson Bay, fur traders spread across the continent, seeking fresh supplies as old ones were exhausted. Alexander Mackenzie, Samuel Hearne, David Thompson, and Simon Fraser were all employees of the Hudson's Bay Company or the North West Company, led on by prospects of establishing new posts and obtaining a rich return in furs. At the posts, Indians were encouraged to kill far more animals than they required – especially beaver – and to trade their surplus skins for the white man's tools and fabrics. One beaver skin would buy a pound of tobacco; twelve would buy a gun; and the four short stripes carried on Hudson's Bay blankets indicate their original price in beaver skins.

Many North American mammals have suffered from the fur trade, but for the beaver it was almost disastrous. Throughout much of the continent the little animal was extinguished, and had French and Italian stylists not shifted interest to the silk hat, the beaver might have followed the dodo, the great

Above: *This close-up of raccoon hair shows the density of the protection provided.*
Right: *The mountain goat's coat is particularly well suited to its environment. The shaggy overcoat lies over a soft, woolly undercoat which protects it from strong winds and cold.*

auk, Steller's sea cow, and others to man-made oblivion.

The thick fur which the hatters of Europe found so desirable is actually only the inner half of the beaver's coat. A typical fur-bearer, the beaver also has longer, coarser guard hairs which overlie the inner coat and protect it. Garments made by native peoples from beaver fur and worn with the hair next to the skin were not considered comfortable until these guard hairs had been worn away. Generally speaking, the colder the climate the richer the fur. Prime beaver pelts are found where the average yearly temperature is below thirty-five degrees. Like the polar bear, the seal, and other aquatic mammals, the beaver will build up layers of fat as required, thus both providing further insulation and increasing its buoyancy; its first line of defence against cold, however, is its coat.

20

So dense is the pelage of the muskox, a unique and ancient ruminant, that it effectively protects him not only against cold but against insects as well. His genetic selection for a short tail arose from his lack of need for a fly swatter, and as an attempt to conserve heat by reducing the size of appendages. Only his nose is exposed. In Eskimo he is called Umingmak, 'the bearded one.' So long and shaggy are the muskox's guard hairs, and so thick is his undercoat, that should he be exposed to a day of freezing rain he will sometimes be brought to his knees under the weight of ice. With the coming of the Arctic summer, however, the muskox, like most mammals living in changing climates, moults much of his undercoat. This wool is called *qiviut* (kee-vee-oot). It is equal to the finest *pashm* from the cashmere goat, and since each beast drops five to six pounds of wool a year (as compared to six ounces of cashmere per goat) a northern cottage industry has recently sprung up in gathering the qiviut and knitting it into clothing. From the qiviut shed by a single animal, one could make three almost weightless sweaters; a scarf four feet long and sixteen inches wide weighs less than one ounce.

---

4 SPECIALIZED GLANDS

For some mammals – those who live in hot climates – the shedding of the undercoat has become permanent, and only a vestigal covering remains. In some instances, species have selected for almost total hairlessness. The whale prefers its insulating blubber, and the rhinoceros has shed all clothing but the cone of agglutinated hair which is its horn.

Mammals which keep their hair have evolved other cooling devices. Most common of these are tiny, synchronized skin muscles which raise the hair like a form-fit venetian blind,

Steller sea lions lack the protective undercoat that many mammals have acquired to serve as added insulation against cold and water.

allowing warm air to escape and trapped moisture to evaporate. The tingling in the neck and scalp during moments of fright is likely an ancient signal that we should be cooled either for flight or combat. Sweat is another cooling device. Men and horses, of course, sweat very heavily, and it was once believed that the hippopotamus actually 'sweated blood' for his flanks are often bathed in a red and oily substance. This secretion cools, protects, and lubricates the hippopotamus's tough hide

For the hippo, good grooming consists of taking frequent baths, but furred mammals must pay careful attention to their coats. As they do so they ingest the vitamin D which has accumulated on the hairs. In this way (and by absorbing it directly through the skin) a sunning squirrel or woodchuck may store enough vitamin D in its liver to last for several months.

Burrs and other foreign bodies in a beaver's coat could quickly destroy its vital waterproofing, and they must be promptly removed. The beaver has the perfect tool for the job – a split, tweezer-like nail on the second toe of each hind foot, which works with the other nails to make a highly efficient comb. Waterproofing is restored partly by drawing on the reserves of special oil glands tucked inside the beaver's ventral opening, partly by stimulating oil glands at the roots of the hairs themselves. If you have ever brushed a dog you will be familiar with the light film of oil which spreads over the coat as you work, giving the animal a sleek and healthy appearance. This oil comes from sebaceous glands in the skin, and although most mammals have them, some are more generously supplied than others. The beaver has many but the fox has few, and for this reason the fox shuns both the rain and the wind which blows his fur aside and penetrates to the skin.

In mammalian evolution, hair and specialized skin glands are inextricably linked. If the fur coat was to do its proper job of insulating against cold it must be water resistant; and if the animal were to be cooled in hot weather evaporation was essential. Hence, sebaceous glands and sweat glands likely evolved very close together. But there are other skin glands even more typical of mammals, and from which the class has derived its name; these are, of course, the mammaries.

Relief from pests

Grazing animals are particularly susceptible to attack from insects. They stand still for long periods of time, and unless they have long tails to swish, they are helpless to ward off their tormentors.

Many animals form mutually beneficial relationships with other species. These symbiotic relationships provide advantages for both species. The magpie in the photograph above is feeding on the parasitic insects carried by the sheep. In this way, the sheep is relieved of its unwelcome guests, and the magpie has a good meal.

Bisons have long, thick hair covering them from shoulders to feet, but their hind quarters have little protection. Flies and mosquitoes, therefore, find these areas particularly enticing. Birds often aid the bison in the same way as they do sheep. But more often, the bison, to find relief from pests, drops to its knees and rolls over and over in the dust, just as the bison at right is doing. The bison will often continue to roll until he has excavated an area that may be up to ten feet across and a couple of feet deep. If this area later becomes filled with water, it will become a delightful mud bath for some itchy bull.

At close range the female manatee is no one's idea of a mermaid. Her blunt snout is covered with bristles, her forehead slopes alarmingly, and her 'grin' is far from intelligent. Nonetheless, manatees and dugongs of the order Sirenia likely stimulated the mermaid legend. Why? Because their breasts resemble women's and they cradle their young like human mothers.

In sexual attraction, mating, and nourishment of young, the experience of mammals is more varied than that of any other class, and in these areas evolution has made its most precise and fascinating experiments.

In most ways the beaver is a very sophisticated mammal. He calculates water levels, builds houses, digs canals, and cooperates to construct dams which may be more than half a mile long. He is monogamous. When they are born in May, his three or four kits are carefully nourished from the mother's breasts and raised with a fondness and indulgence which is surpassed only by the walrus and, among men, equalled only by the Eskimos and the Polynesians. Despite his ancient lineage he seems to be among the most highly developed of mammals; yet, in one respect, he is the most primitive. He has only one vent, a cloaca, which serves for all excretory, generative, and scent-dispensing functions. Unless the female is lactating it is impossible to distinguish between the sexes.

Hidden in this cloaca are two musk glands, each the size of a clenched fist. These are the castors. Their excretions are used to mark boundaries and to communicate in other ways with other beavers. Many animals have similar glands, and some, such as the muskrat and the musk deer, derive their names from them. The scent glands of the muskox are located below his eyes, and the musk is spread when the animal stamps and paws at his face. The antelope is generously supplied with musk glands in various spots all over its body and used, apparently, for different purposes. The skunk's notorious musk glands can be aimed like small turrets, either independently or together. The beaver's musk is called castoreum, and it was once highly valued both as a medicine and as a perfume. Even today, together with musk from a Himalayan deer, civet from an Abyssinian wildcat, and ambergris from the intestine of the sperm whale,

Above: *The manatee is an unlikely mermaid, but its habit of clasping its suckling young like a human mother may have been the origin of the mermaid myth.*
Right: *The presence of mammary glands is unique to mammals. They enable the mother to nurture her young immediately following birth with a readily available source of food. Different methods of suckling are seen here. The duckbilled platypus (top) has mammary glands spread over its abdomen. The opossum keeps her young in a pouch where they suckle for many months. The most common method of suckling is seen in the giraffe, a placental mammal.*

castoreum is one of the most important 'animal notes' used to give a primitive sexual aura to perfumes.

The beaver's multi-purpose cloaca is a sensible adaptation for an aquatic mammal. The sperm of carnivores, ungulates, and primates must be kept cool in special scrotums, and they have lost the squirrel's ability to retract its testicles if danger threatens. Like the whale, the beaver can afford to carry all its reproductive organs safely tucked inside.

5 END OF EGG-LAYING

One order of mammals takes its name from their cloaca. These are the Monotremes (Greek: *mono*, one; *trema*, hole), oldest of all mammals. Only two families remain: the ant-eaters of Australia, Tasmania, and New Guinea, and the duckbilled platypus.

The platypus is a fascinating creature. His rubbery bill is no mere decoration but an extremely efficient tool for prodding grubs out of Australian riverbanks; the female lays flexible reptilian eggs which are joined together to prevent their rolling from the nest; the male has poisonous spurs on his hind legs which are used to subdue the female during copulation, as well as for defence, and he thus shares with the shrew the distinction of being the only poisonous mammals. Most curious, however, is the fact that the milk glands are spread over the female's abdomen, and not concentrated into breasts with a duct through a single nipple. At feeding time the mother simply lies on her back and the young platypuses lap the milk from the pores of the mammary area. Although this arrangement has obvious advantages for a small creature with a duck's bill, the platypus nevertheless represents a very early stage of mammalian development – displaying some post-natal care and nourishment but without the more developed mammary glands of placental animals. Its lineage probably reaches back for 150 million years.

By then, mammals had begun to select quality over quantity in their offspring. The ability to regulate their body temperatures meant that they could move about at night as well as during the day, and that they had more habitats available. This in turn meant changes in the structure of the brain, as new experiences challenged old instincts. Learning became

Twin young, born in spring, are the norm for deer. Shortly after birth, the baby mule deer is able to walk and must nurse within the first hour. Thereafter, it is left alone except for mealtimes. While unattended, it will lie almost motionless for hours in the brush or grass.

29

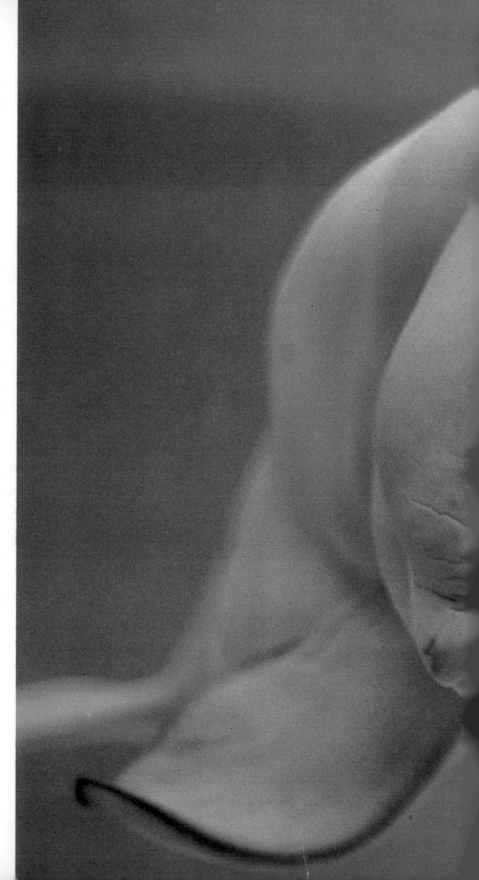

more important for survival, and if the young mammal was to develop and mature properly it needed a longer period of maternal custody. Abandoning egg-laying was a crucial step for mammals, and it was probably taken by two different groups at about the same time – the marsupials and the placentals.

Both experiments have been successful and both are continuing today, although where the two types have competed the placentals have been triumphant. Marsupials are found today mainly in Australia, where they were isolated by the disappearance of the land bridge to Asia one hundred million years ago, and where their development has paralleled that of Eurasian and North American placental types. In Australia there are marsupial wolves, cats and badgers, squirrels and flying squirrels, bears, otters, moles, and rodents. There was once even a rhinoceros-size rabbit called the *Diprotodon*.

Marsupial motherhood requires not only a womb but a portable nursery (Latin: *marsupium*, pouch). Some, like the kangaroo, have large bags, some have small cups, and some have mere flaps of skin. Born after a very short gestation period (eight to forty days), the young scramble up into the pouch and fasten on a teat within. The kangaroo assists her newborn by licking a path through her fur. If there are more babies than teats, the slowest perish. The opossum, the only Canadian marsupial, has thirteen teats but may have as many as eighteen young, each about the size of a honeybee. A kind of link between the marsupials and the monotremes is provided by the spiny anteater, which actually lays an egg that it carries in a pouch until it hatches.

Mobility for the mother and training for the young are the two great benefits offered by marsupial reproduction. At first glance, the placental method of birth, in which the embryo is surrounded in the womb by a sheath of membranes similar to those in a reptile's egg, would seem to offer no advantage. Through the placenta, however, the

Whales are in all respects typically mammalian in their reproduction. The young is nourished in the uterus by a placenta and, after birth, by its mother's milk.

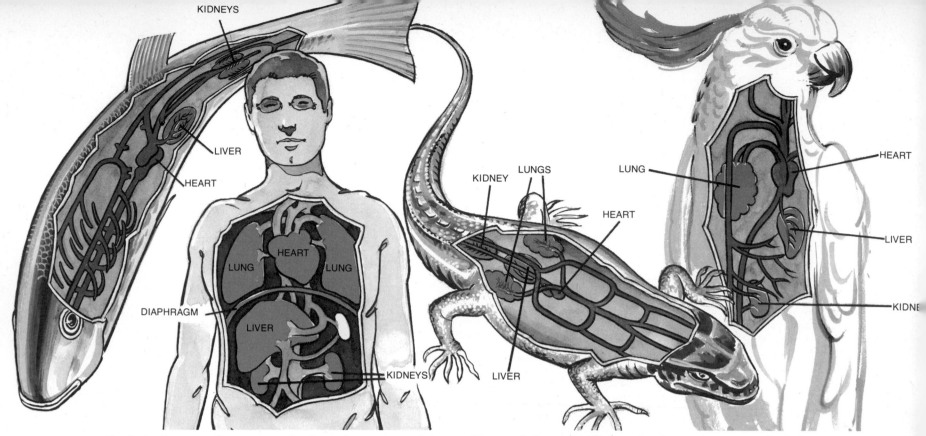

Labels in illustration: KIDNEYS, LIVER, HEART, HEART, LUNG, LUNG, DIAPHRAGM, LIVER, KIDNEYS, KIDNEY, LUNGS, HEART, LIVER, LUNG, HEART, LIVER, KIDNEY

mother's body not only removes the foetus's waste products and provides virtually unlimited energy in return, it also asserts the best possible biological guarantee that delicate systems will develop properly. This fact seems to have played a major part in refining those systems as well as perpetuating them.

Mammals have an efficient circulatory system in which there is a complete separation of aerated from impure blood, and a four-chambered heart, like that of the birds.

6 MEETING NEW NEEDS

No physiological events were more important to mammals than the development of the four-chambered heart and the diaphragm. Both these changes are pre-figured in the crocodile, the most advanced of living reptiles, but other reptiles rely on a sluggish and comparatively inefficient circulatory system. Their three-chambered hearts mix venous and arterial blood, thus reducing the value of oxygen in the latter.

Individual adaptations occur constantly. As well as being a living fossil, every individual is a kind of scout for his species; but in mammals special changes occur only over very long periods of time. Millions of years were required to evolve the mammalian separation of veins and arteries – millions of years, and no doubt, hundreds of thousands of experiments. What occurred was no comparatively minor change in the shape of an extremity or the pigmentation of skin cells, but a fundamental organic restructuring. Increased mobility led to greater demands on muscles, demands relayed back to the brain and answered by the dispatching of more oxygen. This meant larger lungs and a more efficient mechanism for filling them. The mammalian diaphragm is no mere partition separating organs; it is a flat, muscular wall which contracts with inhalation and increases the air capacity of the chest cavity. Together, heart, lungs, and diaphragm function to cleanse the blood and to keep it circulating.

Various species have adapted this equipment according to the requirements of their environments. Risk of frozen extremities confronts every Arctic mammal, and the polar bear's response has been predictable – he has simply thickened his coat. The pads of his feet are bordered by dense, insulating mats of fur. The wolf's foot pad, however, is even more sophisticated. It has a mass of capillaries very near the surface, together with a marvellous thermostatic regulator which circulates just enough warm blood to keep the pad from freezing. Although the snow may be colder than thirty-five degrees below zero, and although the rest of his body may be comfortably warm within its fur coat, yet the wolf conserves his energy by keeping his toes no warmer than they absolutely have to be.

Hibernation is another heat-conserving method used by many Canadian mammals. The woodchuck's normal temperature of 96.8 degrees drops during hibernation to thirty-eight, just above freezing, and his already languid breathing rate of five to seven respirations per minute drops to a mere one breath every six minutes.

Among aquatic mammals, the beaver's cardio-vascular

This hibernating ground squirrel required just over four hours to arouse, during which time its temperature rose from just above freezing to almost 100°F.

and respiratory systems most perfectly suit him for his style of life. Only whales and some seals have greater underwater endurance. An otter, though quick, will drown within four minutes, and although a walrus can dive to 300 feet he can only stay down about ten minutes. The beaver, by contrast, is equipped with massive lungs and an oversized filtering liver. He is remarkably tolerant of carbon dioxide. As he dives his heartbeat slows, and he is able to travel half a mile under water, staying submerged for as long as fifteen minutes. When he surfaces, as he usually does for at least three minutes at a time, his diaphragm operates with extraordinary efficiency. Man exchanges about 15 to 20 per cent of the contents of his lungs every time he exhales and inhales, whereas the beaver exchanges at least 75 per cent. In addition, the beaver has learned to 'wash' his air. Usually, water levels drop slightly after freeze-up, leaving a layer of breathable air, but should the beaver find himself trapped under ice and unable to find an air pocket, he simply dives and exhales. Enough carbon dioxide is filtered out of the rising air, and enough oxygen is picked up from the water, that when the beaver has followed the air to the surface he is able to rebreathe it.

Such a feat, with the blend of reason and instinct which it suggests, draws attention to the last and most awesome of major mammalian characteristics – the enlarged brain.

7 THOUGHT OR INSTINCT

Controlling the muscles which raise and lower hair, and which open and close the sweat and sebaceous glands, are nerves which are part of the peripheral nervous system. Thousands of nerves radiate throughout the body carrying messages to and from the brain via the spinal cord. They are composed of two types of cells: the sensory cells pass ingoing information; the motor cells send orders out. Nerves are therefore two-way streets.

Much of the body's functioning is carried out automatically through this network, although operations such as respiration and excretion may be modified consciously to some extent. All is regulated by the brain. Respiratory and cardiac control centres are located in a portion of the brain called the medulla, which is actually an enlargement of the spinal column. Since these functions are the most fundamental to life, centralized control of them was very likely a first step taken by emergent vertebrates. Organization of all the complex operations of other organs such as the stomach, adrenal glands, kidneys, and so on, is the responsibility of the cerebellum, the 'little brain.' Actually the second largest structure of the nervous system in man, the cerebellum coordinates muscular activity and feeds information on into the thalamus. In Latin, *thalamus* means antechamber, and this portion of the brain is so named because it leads into the much larger cerebrum. The thalamus is the supreme correlation centre. All sensory data are integrated here and forwarded to the frontal lobe, seat of motor control and of planning and foresight.

Structurally the mammalian brain differs hardly at all from that of other vertebrates. Relationships between parts of the brain may vary from shark to lizard, and from lizard to opossum, but the separate responsibilities of the parts remain constant. As mammalian evolution proceeds, however, a section of the brain which is very small in the lizard and almost nonexistent in the shark, begins to grow and to assume greater responsibility. This is the cerebrum, wrapped by the cerebral cortex, where memories are stored and where true thinking – as opposed to instinctual response – occurs. As animals ascend the evolutionary scale, more and more decisions are made in the cerebral cortex, and the cortex grows accordingly. (Or, as the cortex grows, so grows the potential for making decisions.) Many species of ungulates and carnivores show evidence of reason, and in elephants and porpoises the cerebral cortex is very highly developed, requiring most of the one-quarter of total body oxygen intake allocated to the brain.

In man the hemispheres of the cerebral cortex have grown to an enormous size, enfolding the older parts of the brain with millions of cells of dense, convoluted grey matter. Creases in the cortex are as individualistic as fingerprints. They seem to develop in random patterns, and are a device for providing more surface area within a limited space. If our cerebral hemispheres were as smooth as those of a frog, we would need pumpkin-size heads to accommodate them.

Man's cerebral cortex has taken over from the thalamus much of the responsibility for foresight, planning, and motor activity. A squirrel stores nuts because it is driven by an instinctual urge to do so. Man may feel that same urge, but whether he responds to it or not is a decision involving many factors. Reason has therefore not necessarily replaced instinct, but it has wrapped it with absorbing possibilities. Hamlet's

The cougar is the only long-tailed cat native to Canada. It prefers wild, rugged country and has, therefore, been restricted in its range by the growth of civilization.

tragedy is agonizingly human: he must think before he acts.

Millions of years, innumerable mutations, myriad adaptations – these have brought man to his position of apparent dominance over other animals. If he is a hunter or a trapper he can outsmart them; if he is a farmer he can domesticate them. Should they interfere with his objectives he will eradicate without scruple the last members of once-populous species. Only rarely does he pause to consider that although he differs superficially from other mammals, his resemblances to them stretch back through countless generations. His highly articulated arm and hand, and his opposable thumb, are the legacy of shrew-like and lemur-like ancestors; his invaluable ability to perceive depth is the result of mutations which steadily brought the eyes forward until their fields of vision overlapped; and buried deep at the center of his brain, influencing his massive cortex with emotions he cannot comprehend, lies the elusive limbic system, the ancient smell-brain of mammals long since vanished.

Extinction is not new in nature. Two-thirds of known species no longer exist, and for each animal for which we have a fossil record there may well be a dozen more unknown to science. Most perished not because they were inadequately adapted but, on the contrary, because they were over-specialized and could not change with changing circumstances. During 2,000 years in North America, so far as is known, only one species became extinct, but in the century between 1850 and 1950 about thirty species became extinct. In the last twenty years, the pace has accelerated yet again. Throughout the world we have eliminated one species of animal for every year of this century, and 1,000 species of vertebrates are now endangered.

Not long ago, Canada had few animals not found elsewhere in the world – the Gaspé shrew, the red-backed vole and Vancouver marmot of British Columbia, and some types of a little mouse-like creature called the Phenacomys. So devastating have been man's recent activities in the United States, however, that Canada has become a sanctuary for animals whose range was once much larger. Among them are the bison, the moose, the woodland caribou, the lynx, the cougar, and the muskox.

Will they find refuge here, or are their prospects dim? The record of Canadian conservation – even in the far north – is not encouraging. When Europeans first arrived in the north, there may have been as many as five million barren-ground caribou roaming free. For perhaps 25,000 years they had filled the needs of man without serious depletion of the herds – a tent took twenty hides, a kayak ten, a suit of clothing seven, and a sleeping bag six. By 1960 that herd of five million had been reduced to 250,000, and the caribou was on its way to joining other seriously threatened species – the northern fox; the glacier bear, the polar bear, and the barren-ground grizzly; the sea otter and the Atlantic walrus; the big-horn sheep, the black-footed ferret, and the eastern panther.

Man may believe that reason has carried him beyond the ecological controls to which all other living things are subject. His habits of killing off his fittest young males in warfare, and of preserving the sick and the weak by medicine, suggest that he thinks he has transcended natural selection. Ironically, however, should man persist in his proliferation and in his drastic simplifications of his environment, he will threaten his own survival, for with each habitat destroyed, with each species obliterated, he reduces the marvellous diversity through which nature has produced him and on which he depends. Variety and complexity make stable environments. By simplifying, man increases the risk of radical changes to which he himself might not adapt. Should man's activities precipitate a global catastrophe, then his huge brain will have proved to be an over-specialization, and reason will have become a liability. Natural selection will again function with its pitiless wisdom, and the earth will be given to more dependable forms of life. Perhaps the platypus, the opossum, and the beaver who were present at our birth shall witness our passing too; and if none of our survivors bears a warming coat and suckles offspring, then, like the age of dinosaurs before it, the age of mammals will have reached an end.

When the first white man reached this continent, millions of bison ranged from Great Slave Lake to New Mexico. Today they survive in refuges like Wood Buffalo Park, Alberta.

WAYLAND DREW

PART TWO
THE PEAK OF EVOLUTION

The advent of the first mammals was a quiet, unobtrusive evolutionary event that occurred early in the Mesozoic era. At this time the small members of a somewhat mammal-like order of reptiles called Therapsida, skulked through the lush vegetation of tropical swamps. The therapsids (who had themselves descended from an earlier reptilian order, the Pelycosauria) soon developed a number of mammalian characteristics, one of which may have been a body covering of hair. Dr Robert Broom's excavations in South Africa in 1897 turned up specimens of the therapsids which revealed a mixture of reptilian and mammalian characteristics, including possession of a secondary palate, which enables the animal to breathe while eating – a mammalian trait. Gone were the peg-like teeth of the reptiles. Instead Broom found well-defined incisors, canines, and molars, and legs articulating out from under the body to hoist the belly up from the ground

The pygmy shrew, Canada's smallest mammal, belongs to one of the oldest orders of mammals. All mammals are probably evolved from small, insectivorous animals similar to the shrew.

for running – an improvement over the side-legged, belly-dragging gait of the reptiles. This primitive order of mammals became extinct during the latter part of the Triassic period in the face of constant competition from the predominant dinosaurs. Mammals survived unobtrusively for the next fifty million years by remaining small, inconspicuous (very likely nocturnal), and non-competitive. Having acquired hair and the beginnings of the ability to regulate their own body temperatures, they began to exploit the occasional biological vacuums left by the dinosaurs in their enforced retreat from the cooling northern limits of their ranges.

There were other advantages to be exploited. The evolution away from egg-laying to the bearing of live young also conveyed real benefits, especially in the colder climate. Earlier vertebrates had relied on laying a great many eggs in order to ensure the survival of the few young required to replace each year's dying adults. Fishes spawned their eggs in thousands, amphibians typically in hundreds. The reptiles improved on this, for apart from the innovation of laying shelled eggs, they probably also added a measure of nest protection, as do some modern snakes and crocodiles. If so, then

39

even fewer eggs were needed. Now, however, the first mammals had evolved the ultimate in parental protection: the retention of the egg by the female and its internal fertilization by the male. Doubtless, the first step in the process was the provision of food by the development of mammary glands.

The next mammalian order to evolve, the Marsupialia, dispensed completely with egg-laying. Marsupials produce tiny, easily-born young which climb into an abdominal pouch to suckle and grow until mature enough to venture forth. Most marsupials are now found in Australia. The only marsupial found in North America is the opossum – a Mesozoic animal, essentially unchanged in 100 million years. In later mammalian orders came the modern mode of producing fewer but larger young, which are retained internally until their advanced development and size require their birth.

Mammals thus achieved a method of reproduction of great economy, and one that protects the young when they need it most. Such adaptations would give the emerging class great advantages over the reptiles whose eggs could freeze, and whose only means of temperature regulation was to move with the sun's heat. Add to the mammals' cold-weather nimbleness their developing brain power and the stage was set for mammalian ascendency.

Some distinctly mammalian skeletal characteristics also evolved. The vertebral column of the trunk was now divided between a rigidly articulated thoracic (chest) region, which served to support the ribs, and a lumbar region, which was highly flexible. In all mammals the motion of the trunk is centred on the lumbar region, which is so constructed as to allow powerful up-and-down movement. Thus, mammals progress by flexing the vertebral column in the vertical plane. This is true of even the sea-going mammals, including the mighty whales, whose flukes are placed horizontally.

The young of the opossum, the only North American marsupial, are poorly developed at birth, but have remarkably strong forelimbs with which they climb along their mother's body to a teat. Opossums are tree-climbing animals and have a prehensile tail and five fully developed toes on each foot.

41

The evolution of the horse

The evolution of the horse from Eohippus *to the modern-day* Equus *took about 60 million years. In the process, each succeeding form was more adapted to running long distances in open, level country and to eating the grass of the prairies. The increasing height, and the reduction of the number of toes, gave the animal more speed. The horses here are* (left to right) Eohippus, Orohippus, Mesohippus, Merychippus, *and* Equus.

The cooler climates and seasonal fluctuations, which typified the late Cretaceous period, brought to a close the great age of the reptiles. The big dinosaurs probably disappeared first from the northern extremities of their range in Siberia and Canada, retreating before the cold to make their last stand in the tropics. Unable to adapt quickly enough to the changes in their environment they perished, leaving the stage to the early mammals who now possessed all the requirements for expansion.

The ascent of the mammals was a slow process at first, but it gathered momentum as the Paleocene epoch opened. As the dinosaurs died out, the small, furry, insectivorous early mammals gave rise (by the process of adaptive radiation) to an array of mammalian species which included the ancestors of all of today's nineteen orders, and many others that have since become extinct. Mammals expanded into the ecological spaces made available to them by the declining reptiles. With their superior survival equipment – larger brains, more efficient breeding methods and heat regulation – mammals could now compete actively with *all* existing forms of life. This was truly the age of mammals, wherein only the completely successful non-mammal could be allowed to survive.

Curiously, the mammals are second only to the amphibians in the small number of species they represent. This paucity can be understood, however, when one realizes that as a class they tend to occupy positions of dominance over earlier forms. It is less their role to be eaten than to do the eating. But they do not all dominate. Every animal survives within certain, often narrow limits, which ecologists term the animal's 'niche.' Wherever a reptile or bird has successfully occupied a given niche and has been able to withstand mammalian competition for it, the original occupant likely still survives.

8 SURVIVAL OF THE FITTEST

In order to demonstrate the evolutionary processes at work in North America since the mammals evolved into their dominant position, one specific group may serve as an example. The family Equidae includes the modern domesticated horse, its wild cousins, and many extinct forms which were important as stages in the evolution of the present-day horse. Their development began in the Eocene 60 million years ago, with *Eohippus* – the dawn horse – a short-necked animal the size of a cat, with four front toes and three hind toes. Large numbers of this little animal browsed in the lush tropical forests. By the beginning of the Oligocene, 40 million years ago, with its trend toward drying and cooler temperatures, the descendants of *Eohippus* had grown to twice the original size, and were beginning to adapt to life out on the spreading grasslands. To this end, they continued to develop length of leg and with it, more speed. This slightly more horse-like creature

was *Mesohippus*.

Picture the North American scene at the opening of the Miocene, 30 million years ago. The grasslands are still extending, the forests shrinking. Out on the edge of the prairies the herds of sheep-sized *Mesohippus* browse, their only defence against carnivores being their speed. Then somewhere, doubtless as the result of a chance mutation, an animal with considerably longer legs and taller stature appears. It can see farther and run faster than its peers. The simple Darwinian principle of the survival of the fittest works to ensure its survival, and that of its long-legged offspring. Thus did *Mesohippus* give rise to its successor *Merychippus*. Within eight million years the sheep-sized *Mesohippus* was gone, completely replaced by the pony-sized *Merychippus*.

The Pliocene epoch began 13 million years ago, and was characterized in North America by an increasingly arid climate. Under this influence, the horse line developed still further toward its present state by adapting exclusively to grazing as a food gathering technique. During this epoch, ancestral horses gained in size and speed, and their toes finally gave way to hooves. Thus there emerged the fore-

runner of the modern horse – *Pliohippus*. The latter-day *Equus*, destined to be first tamed then domesticated by early man, belongs to the Pleistocene and comparatively recent times; its entire history covers no more than a million years. However, although the horse had largely evolved in North America, these latter events were destined to take place in the old world. At the onset of the Ice Age, the horse inexplicably died out in North America. However, those herds that had migrated west across the Bering land bridge to Eurasia prior to the onset of glaciation survived to give rise to the modern genus *Equus*, which includes Africa's zebras Asia's wild horses, and north Africa's wild asses. The Spanish explorers who landed in the Americas in the sixteenth century brought the horse back to North America with them. It was from escapees of this stock that the Indians acquired the wild 'mustang' of the western prairies.

The camel is also to a great extent a product of the climatic and evolutionary factors of the North American continent. Their recognizable ancestors appeared here 50 million years ago. *Protylopus* was four-toed and not much larger than a jackrabbit. From this beginning, camels began to evolve in several ways. Most grew larger, although a few remained small. They very rapidly lost their side toes and became two-toed animals; their legs increased in length, and the neck, of necessity, lengthened, since they had to stoop to graze. Fifteen million years ago all camels resembled modern llamas. Although the South American forms have remained similar to their ancestors, the rest have grown even taller and evolved the fat-storing hump and other desert-living specializations. Modern camels and llamas went their own evolutionary ways in North America until after the advent of the Ice Age. A few camels travelled west to Asia, some of the llamas migrated south over the land bridge to South America, but most of them appear to have remained in North America, and here, due to unknown factors, they became extinct during the Pleistocene.

The bulldozing effect of the great glaciers destroyed much

The wild horses of Sable Island are believed to be the descendants of domestic animals from wrecked ships. Over the centuries, the breed has regressed to a typical short wild animal.

of the Canadian fossil record of early mammals. However, there are some notable exceptions. Dr Richard C. Fox of the University of Edmonton has uncovered in the Upper Cretaceous rock formations of Alberta a rich fossil record of early mammals which were contemporaries of the declining dinosaurs. Most of these early mammals were small. During Tertiary times a rich and varied mammalian fauna particularly rich in herbivores flourished in North America. Dr Loris Russell of the Royal Ontario Museum has collected a particularly fine skull of *Archaeotherium*, a cow-sized, pig-like omnivore of the Oligocene epoch from the Cypress Hills region of Saskatchewan.

Sharing the Canadian landscape with the horses and camels were the rhinoceros, the elephant, and the hippopotamus. Rhinos remained common in North America right up until the Pliocene when they dwindled and became extinct. In Europe, the woolly rhinoceros survived until the Pleistocene, while in Asia and Africa, related species survive to this day.

9 EMERGENCE OF MAN

Prior to these events and during the latter part of the Cenozoic era, the ancestors of present-day apes and men were flourishing in African forests. The possession of a superior brain had been a vital factor in the mammals' rise to ascendency over the other classes, and this order – the Primates – above all others was singularly well endowed. In time, it would come to dominate all other mammals.

Modern lemurs, tarsiers, marmosets, baboons, spider monkeys, gorillas and humans are all Primates, and their line goes back to the Paleocene, 70 million years ago. All have flattened or cupped nails on long fingers and toes, and an opposable thumb on each hand. This adaptation, originally for climbing, also enables them to grasp an object in the palm of the hand. Heads are large and brains well developed. Three-dimensional vision is achieved with the two frontally placed eyes, whose fields of vision overlap. There is a single pair of mammary glands in the thoracic region. The Primate line began with a small arboreal insectivorous mammal similar to a modern tree shrew. The early Primates were all insectivorous or herbivorous tree dwellers, well adapted to survive in their arboreal niches. There was little in their origin to suggest their ultimate destiny. Rather than revealing any high degree of specialization, it was their singular lack of such that might be said to have distinguished them. Theirs was, in fact, a decidedly general-purpose kind of anatomy. Herein lay much of their ultimate success; for versatility combined with brain power was to prove unbeatable. Lemurs evolved early, followed by the bug-eyed tarsiers; next came the new and old world monkey families. Some new world monkeys, such as the spider monkey, have long prehensile tails on which they can swing, Old world monkeys, like the baboons, have small, relatively useless tails. Later came the heavier anthropoids, living most of their lives on the ground but retreating readily to the trees for safety or sleep. As the African climate changed increasingly in favour of grasslands during the Miocene and into the Pliocene, a major split occurred in the higher Primate line. Some, like *Ramapithecus*, took to the open savannahs, to walk progressively more erect, to use weapons and tools to survive primarily as hunters. Others stayed with the retreating forests, and their present-day, largely herbivorous descendants, the chimpanzee and the gorilla, still cling to their final strongholds in the forest remnants. These man-like higher Primates had much larger and better developed cerebrums than the smaller earlier Primates. Intelligence has increased steadily among the Primates and today's chimpanzee is a highly intelligent animal. But there is a distinct gap between the intelligence of ape and of man. The gorilla's brain size, for example, does not exceed 635 cubic centimetres, whereas man's comes close to 2,000.

Prehistoric man emerged into the climatic fluctuations of the Pleistocene in Europe as a skilled and intelligent hunter. There is much scientific speculation as to precisely what part he played, if any, in the extinction of the larger Pleistocene mammals. Their demise in the old world occurred about 25,000 years ago; in the new world about 9,000 years ago. On both sides of the Atlantic, primitive man was on hand to witness their passing. The earliest firm evidence of early

man in North America is a very recent find: a fleshing tool manufactured from the tibia of a caribou. It was excavated in 1966 near Old Crow in the northern Yukon and recently reported on jointly by Dr W. N. Irving of the University of Toronto and C. R. Harrington of the National Museums of Canada. This artifact together with associated mammoth leg bones, thought to have been smashed by stone-hammers, have radiocarbon dates of approximately 27,000 years before the present. This new evidence definitely establishes the presence of man on this continent before the peak of the last glaciation.

A milestone of primitive cultural evolution was the development of a social organization. Sub-tribal hunting bands

were formed earlier in Europe than in North America. The development of speech and the discovery of fire were dramatic achievements that greatly aided man in his evolutionary ascent. The same torches that lit the Cro Magnon caves, enabling those early artists to decorate their walls with animal paintings, were also used as weapons to drive these same animals to their deaths. Torches were waved to panic the herding animals and grass fires were set to cause their stampede. It is unlikely that such fires, once started, were ever put out by man. The long-term effect could well have been serious habitat destruction. Man's numbers were small however, and it is probable that climatic factors were largely responsible for the great die-offs of the Pleistocene.

The evolution of man

In geological terms, the history of man's evolution is brief. Within the last million years of earth history, man evolved from some ape-like creature to his present form. In the process, man evolved not only his upright stance, but also a larger brain, and hands and feet more suited to life on the ground and his erect position.

Fossil evidence of early man has been found on all continents except the North American, where primates became extinct before they had even reached the monkey stage. Man re-entered the New World at a later date, probably from Asia.

10 TWO-WAY TRAFFIC

The Pleistocene began about two million years ago. Since the end of the Mesozoic era, 60 million years ago, there had been a steady decline in world temperature, which culminated in a sharp drop at the beginning of the Pleistocene. Throughout the Cenozoic the cooling and drying trends resulted in the formation of the glaciers which typified the Pleistocene. Cooling temperatures alone did not produce the ice ages; large amounts of precipitation were also required. The drying up of southerly latitudes put the moisture into the earth's atmosphere, which in turn provided the precipitation to create the dramatic ice formations occurring at their greatest extent in Canada. Progressively each summer, the winter's snow persisted, and the polar caps thickened and spread. Glaciers advanced over the landscape.

During the warmer interglacial periods (of which there were at least four), the climate over much of North America and Eurasia was temperate or even tropical. The cooling effect of each returning period of glaciation developed slowly, over thousands of years. During these periods northern species extended their ranges to the south. Only those animals with special cold-weather adaptations like the woolly mammoth, which wore dense wool beneath its coarse hair, could remain in the frozen north. At the height of the periods of glaciation, the Bering land bridge (actually a broad, shallow plain) connected the new world to the old and provided a two-way escape route for many of the hardier sub-Arctic mammals, including mammoths, horses, muskoxen, bison, camels, wolves, sabre-tooth cats, and man. Pleistocene mastodons were found only in the Americas, the woolly rhinoceros, the Irish elk, and the cave bear only in Europe. Moose, caribou, muskoxen, mountain sheep, walruses, and the true bears all came to North America over the bridge. During the interglacial periods, South and Central America produced, in their isolation, their own unique mammalian faunas. *Glyptodon*, a huge turtle-like armadillo, was one species; *Megatherium*, a giant ground-living sloth, who could

reach up to twenty feet to browse, was another. At the return of glaciation, with so much of the earth's water locked up in ice, sea levels were lowered 200 to 300 feet, and the great land masses were again connected so that North American species could spread south, and South American species north. The invaders from the south were far from successful in competition with the existing North American species; for most southern invaders the experiment ended in extinction. However, this two-way traffic tended to be beneficial for immigrants from the north like the *Smilodon*, the sabre-tooth cat with eight-inch fangs, and the dire wolf, *Canis dirus*. Both of these carnivores became common in South America, preying upon its many large herbivores.

In a period as climatically catastrophic as the Pleistocene, insurmountable problems faced many animals with insufficient time to adapt. Consider the ill-fated mastodon. Ten feet high at the shoulder this woolly elephant, of which we have abundant fossil evidence, had preceded the mammoth into North America by millions of years. At the end of the last glaciation, temperatures rose and the ice sheets melted back. As summers became warmer and longer, the spruce forests which were a prime food source of the browsing mastodon, steadily retreated northwards. Even now the black spruce tolerates colder temperatures than any other coniferous tree. It can survive in temperatures as low as –70 degrees Fahrenheit. It is not likely that the mastodon could have done so. Thus, progressively, winter temperatures in the spruce forests became critically colder and the mastodons were left with the choice of staying to freeze or moving, only to starve. Forced southward during the winter, they were obliged to expend more energy travelling in search of the sparse food supply than they could gain by finding it. Attempts to utilize alternative food sources did not succeed – resulting in lowered vitality and a heavier winter mortality. It is not known to what extent early North American man hastened this process of extinction, although we do know that he did hunt the mastodon. There is evidence at a site in Michigan of numbers being butchered at one time. A somewhat similar fate could be conjectured for the herds of woolly mammoths which measured nine feet at the shoulder and roamed across the continent during the ice ages.

ASIA

NORTH AMERICA

A land bridge probably formed and receded a number of times during the Pleistocene ice ages. As the glaciers formed, the waters of the oceans were increasingly locked in ice, resulting in a lowering of the water levels, and the exposure of a broad plain between Asia and Alaska (shown in the insert at its widest extent).

Early man probably crossed this plain, as did such animals as the sabre-toothed tiger, the dire wolf, the muskox, the moose, and the bison. Some of these animals became extinct, either as a result of changing climatic conditions or at the hands of man, while others adapted to the changing conditions in North America or moved to more suitable southern areas.

Each time the ice advanced, probably four times within about one million years, dramatic climatic changes took place, forcing the inhabitants of the entire world, and especially the extreme northern and southern regions, to adapt or move.

These changes did not take place quickly, but over thousands of years, as the ice advanced and the ocean levels lowered. The inhabitants of North America were forced to find new food supplies and new surroundings more conducive to survival. Thus, most of our 'native' animals at one time, not too long ago in geological time, made their homes in more regions farther to the south.

Conversely, many animals that we associate with warmer climates, such as elephants and monkeys, once roamed North America.

As one might expect, the variable nature of the Pleistocene placed a premium on adaptability, and stimulated evolutionary development. The effect on the evolution of man was most decisive. Not only did man's greater adaptability become a particular asset in these times, his use of tools also gave him a significant advantage.

11 CANADA'S MIXTURE

Today's Canadian mammals form a mixture composed of the survivors of the Ice Age and recent arrivals from the south, to which we must add those species deliberately or unknowingly introduced by man. The ranges of many of the older mammal inhabitants have greatly decreased in area from those enjoyed in former, more favourable times. The skull of a grizzly bear recovered from a gravel pit near Orillia, Ontario, in 1961 is displayed in the Royal Ontario Museum. Dr Randolph Peterson, curator of mammals, reports its radiocarbon dated age as about 11,700 years. Nowadays, grizzlies are limited to areas in the west. The site of the nation's capital was once part of the Champlain Sea which was formed from the melting Laurentide glacier. The bones of the white whale brought up from a depth of twenty feet out of a sand pit within a half-mile of Ottawa's Uplands airport are approximately 10,420 years old. Harp seal bones of similar antiquity have also come from sandy deposits in the Ottawa region.

We have retained our beavers in spite of heavy trapping since Europeans pioneered in North America. But *Castoroides ohioensis* – a seven-foot long prehistoric beaver – became extinct before the last retreat of the ice. In the 1890s Dr William Brodie found its bones at depths between fifty and sixty feet in the banks of the Don River near its mouth in Toronto. They were accompanied by the remains of bison, a grizzly-type bear, two species of deer, and a woodchuck. They are known to be in excess of 46,000 years old. As the climate continues to ameliorate, recent arrivals from the south have increased the number of Canadian mammals. The bobcat

The mammoth, which roamed in North America during the Pleistocene age, was hunted by early man. Although it emerged on earth at about the same time as the ancestors of today's elephants, it disappeared about 10,000 years ago. The inserts show a Gnathobelodon with two tusks and a spoon-shaped lower lip, a Stegodon (the first modern elephant), a mammoth, largest of the elephants, and a modern elephant.

moved into southwestern Ontario about 1880. The brush wolf came from the southwest during the last century, and the common opossum moved into southern Ontario around 1850. Introductions which were deliberate include the European hare or jackrabbit, released in 1912 near Brantford, Ontario, the nutria or coypu, introduced in 1927 as breeding stock for fur farms (from which some later escaped), and of course the familiar domesticated farm mammals. Not all such introductions have been desirable: the Norway or brown rat and the house mouse arrived in North America as common shipboard pests and were thought, as late as 1830, to be confined to the immediate Toronto waterfront. As all Canadians are well aware, this is no longer the case.

Today's mammals range in size from the tiny pygmy shrew, four inches long and the weight of a dime, to the mighty (but threatened) blue whale, the largest animal the world has ever known, measuring more than one hundred feet in length and weighing approximately one ton for every foot. There are about twenty thousand species and sub-species of mammals on earth and palaeontologists, who have diligently studied their prehistory, tell us they represent less than one-third the number known to have been involved in the evolutionary process which produced them; thus for every surviving mammal at least two have become extinct. During the 200 million years since their beginning, mammals have had to contend with great changes in climate and geography, as well as ever-increasing pressures from their own kind. The survival of a species is a complex matter involving many factors. The fossil record shows that a given genus has tended to survive no longer than ten million years before needing to change drastically. Thus, succeeding generations take on different forms and earn new names. The greatest certainty within the evolutionary process is change. Extinction, then, is very much a natural part of the ongoing life process. Man-made extinction, however – especially when caused by the wanton destruction not only of animals themselves, but of entire habitats – must be seen for what it is: a permanent desecration of our earth, perhaps the most immoral act that man or any generation of men can commit.

D. H. BALDWIN

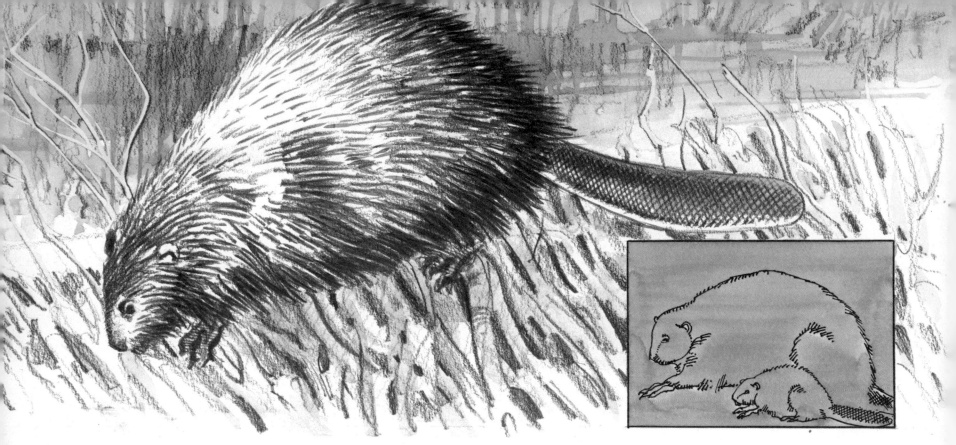

Canada's largest rodent

The beaver is the largest North American rodent, but it is a dwarf compared to its ancestor Castoroides ohioensis (above), which measured at least seven feet long and weighed 800 pounds. The present-day species is about four feet long, of which one-third is tail. The average adult male weighs about fifty pounds.

The beaver has adapted well to its surroundings. Its long, sharp teeth help it to obtain food and materials for shelter. The beaver's diet consists primarily of bark and, in the summer, aquatic plants. A beaver will also stockpile branches for the winter at the bottom of his pond.

A beaver colony, which may contain as many as twelve individuals, typically consists of two adults, several two-year-old offspring, and the young of the current year.

The beaver lodge is built of sticks and mud and contains chambers which open underwater. When the young are born in the spring, the floor of the chamber is lined with rushes. These are replaced as they become soiled.

The ingenuity of the beaver did not protect it from near extinction at the hands of trappers who supplied the European trade with pelts. The dense fur which protects the beaver from cold water was once highly prized. As a result of man's interference, the line which started with Castoroides ohioensis almost ended in the last century.

Just as the whaling fleets subsidized empire in New England, the fur of the beaver was the source of income for great European empires. The beaver once occurred in a large area covering most of North America, but are now more limited in their range.

Canadian naturalist, Bruce Wright, calls the beaver 'a key to wildlife abundance.' The damming up of streams and ponds provides large areas of shallow water for fish and water plants. This in turn attracts more moose and ducks. In order to encourage the beaver in his efforts, man has occasionally moved beavers into an area so that spring flood control can be aided by their dams.

52

PART THREE
VITAL BALANCES

Porcupines love salt. Their craving for it is strongest in the spring, and many die along Canada's highways every year when the first thaws leave crusty accumulations on posts and bridges. As campers and cottage owners well know, even a slight sweat residue on axe handles, paddles, packstraps, boots, saddles, and harnesses is enough to entice a porcupine, and because these rodents never hibernate, man's dwellings are always vulnerable. A porcupine has even been known to gnaw through a thick glass jar to get at the salt inside. Salt, however, is only a spice in the porcupine's diet; the staple is bark, especially the succulent bark of pines.

Normally, porcupines girdle and kill relatively few trees. A day's meal for an adult is a patch of bark about the size of this page. Because they are inveterate wanderers, the damage they inflict tends to be lightly spread over many acres of forest. Their activities are an integral part of woodland life,

Porcupines are armoured with about 30,000 special hairs (quills). They are fond of buds, twigs, and the inner bark of trees, as well as salt.

counterbalancing those of the squirrel who forgets where buried nuts and pine cones are hidden. Dead trees open the forest to new growth and provide nesting sites for insects and for the woodpeckers attracted to them.

Cougars, wolves, and bears will sometimes attack porcupines, but only two predators regularly eat them, and only one depends on porcupine flesh for a large percentage of its diet. Both the bobcat and the fisher enjoy an immunity to the deadly festering that quills cause in other animals. The fisher, moreover, prefers porcupine to any other meat, and it has learned the knack of flicking the little rodent on its back, exposing its vulnerable belly. Even if a fisher should accidently swallow some quills they will pass harmlessly through its intestine; the fisher is admirably equipped, therefore, to help keep porcupines from overbreeding.

The fisher is sleek black-and-silver, an agile predator related to the marten and the weasel. Despite his name he lives mainly on porcupines, rabbits, and squirrels. Unfortunately, his luxurious coat has made him a trapper's prize, and together with lumbering and forest fires, trapping has reduced the Canadian fisher population to only a few thousand. As

the fisher declines the porcupine flourishes. More porcupines eat more trees, posing a serious economic threat to lumbermen, who slaughter them whenever possible. The resulting overkill eliminates a major source of the fisher's food and helps to hurry this elegant predator towards extinction. Having once begun to meddle, man finds that he has blundered like the proverbial bull in the china shop, smashing fragile relationships and balances.

No animal exists in a vacuum. All have evolved in response to their environments, and their lives form part of an elaborate and changing tapestry. Each asserts it in predictable ways, but the behaviour of each is modified by the presence of others. All are affected by the food supply of their habitat; all participate in a profusion of vital checks and tensions. Ecology, the branch of biology that studies these relationships, appropriately derives its name from *oikos*, the Greek word for house.

The balances that existed – before the coming of the white man – among Indians, fishers, porcupines, and forests, were part of a healthy ecosystem stabilized by diversity and by tensions mutually imposed. None dominated; all profited.

Despite its name, the fisher rarely eats fish. Its food consists of a variety of small animals, especially porcupines, which it kills with impunity. Even when quills pierce its skin, they don't cause the usual festering sores. Like its close relative, the marten, the fisher has been depleted in many areas by trappers, with a resulting porcupine-population increase in those regions.

Of course, individual trees were girdled, individual porcupines were eaten, and individual fishers were snared and skinned. At the same time, Indian trappers fell victim to accidents and disease. But the balances among *species* remained more or less constant. In nature, that fact is of prime importance. So long as any species exists it can continue to experiment and to evolve; the more species there are, the more stable all ecosystems will be.

While ecologists look around them at the agreements between species, ethologists look inward, attempting to trace the controlling inheritance, or 'program,' of individual types. Mammals are social creatures. Even solitary wanderers like the wolverine and the lynx must keep contact with other of

56

their kind. Their methods of communication are an integral part of their life styles, essential to feeding, mating, and care of young. Certain aspects of these activities may be learned, but they are mainly instinctual, part of that genetic heritage evolved by the species for its own protection.

Among the most interesting ecological and ethological studies are those which have shown that animals regulate their own populations, and that much social activity is devoted to assessing food supplies. It has long been known that wolf populations level off at a density of one for approximately ten square miles. An even more dramatic example of self-regulation (homeostasis) recently occurred in the Murchison Falls area of Uganda. When crowding threatened an elephant herd in that region, females simply lengthened the period between births from four years to nine. How they did this is uncertain, but a clue may be found in the ability of other females – notably rabbits and muskrats – either to produce fewer embryos or to reabsorb some through the walls of the womb. This happens when the population begins to threaten the carrying capacity of the environment, but before actual shortages occur. Starvation, an extreme and dangerous form of thinning, is thus avoided. Necessary reduction of lion populations occurs through the stern social custom that cubs eat last; in lean times, the young starve. Primitive men used a variety of mechanisms to limit their numbers, including delayed marriage, celibacy, polyandry, abortion, infanticide, and prolonged nursing. In dire conditions of overcrowding, they resorted to the devices of captive animals – fratricide and cannibalism – practices abhorred among widely scattered peoples.

When prolonged, even slight stress and overcrowding cause nervous changes that affect a mammal's ability to reproduce. Fat reserves become depleted; the thymus, spleen, and red blood cells falter; the mammary and reproductive glands malfunction; and the endocrine system may be so impaired that the body's ability to resist disease is ominously reduced. When snowshoe hare populations are not adequately thinned by wolves, foxes, cats, and other natural predators, the crowded survivors appear to grow increasingly neurotic. Their spleens shrink, lesions appear on their adrenal and thyroid glands, and their atrophied livers no longer store the glycogen necessary for normal carbohydrate reserve. Ultimately, they literally die of shock.

Any overpopulation upsets the ecological balance and threatens the overbreeders with starvation. Clearly, then, it is in the interest of any species to regulate its numbers before that point is reached, or before nervous and physical derangements make it vulnerable to disease. Many of the congregations, displays, courtship rituals, hierarchies, and varied communications that comprise social life among mammals apparently aid restraint within the species by providing ways of taking census, assessing food supplies, and assigning breeding privileges. One theory is that mammals – with such exceptions as lemmings, snowshoe hares, and men – take care not to breed themselves into a state of hysterical mass suicide, just as they take care to select mates for the maximum benefit of the species, and to nurture and protect their young.

All of these vital activities require the precise sending and receiving of messages.

12 COMMUNICATIONS

Many signals inadvertently carry beyond the borders of the species. The grumbling of an elephant's belly announces his presence to everyone within a quarter of a mile; a blowing seal may be heard half a mile away; and the distinctive odour of many predators warns their prey. Such signals form part of the network of checks and tensions in a healthy ecological system. Most messages, however, are intended for the mammal's own kind, and they include a great variety of sights, sounds, and smells.

Unlike birds and lizards, most mammals are colour blind. Visual signals are, therefore, less important to them than scent and sound. Some, indeed, like the hapless mole and the myopic shrew, have almost completely abandoned sight in favour of the other senses. Nonetheless, movement, flashing white signals, and expression all play a part in mammalian communication. Buck white-tailed deer, for example, do not usually raise their tails when they run, but the doe's flag seems

Sounds and signals

Mammals often have highly refined methods of communicating and interpreting the messages of their environment. Most of these messages relate to sound, sight, and smell, and may take the form of distinctive noises (like the marmot's chirp), expressive postures (like the wolf's crouch), and identifying odours (like the musk deposited by many mammals).

The menacing stance and expression of the cougar (right) may be enough to warn intruders away. When it is stalking prey, the cougar relies on stealth. Its prey must therefore be alert to the slightest sounds of warning. Thus, the white-tailed deer (far right) has highly developed ears which it can direct towards suspicious sounds. The deer's sense of sight and smell are also keen—an important attribute for the most preyed upon of all our large animals.

The beaver's tail is also used for communication. The reverberating slap serves as a warning of approaching danger. The elk (left) also uses sound to communicate to members of its own group. Here a bull bugles its challenge to other males. The bugle starts low and rises to a clean note, then flattens out to a braying sound. This startling noise can be heard for miles and usually signifies the onset of the breeding season or rut.

to provide a beacon for the fawns as they chase her in the dimly lit forest. The cottontail's puff may serve a similar function.

Because of their general suppleness, mammals have a wide range of expression available. Much of their communication is 'body talk.' Ears can be raised or laid flat; hair can be smoothed or erected; tails can be waved or tucked between the legs; mouth, lips, eyes, and nostrils – all can express defiance, threat, or tenderness; and the stance of the body itself tells a great deal to both friend and foe. A dog with its head low is either hurt or cowed. Threatening postures in which the lips are curled up, the head thrust forward, and the ears laid back, are an unmistakable message implying the ability to hurt, and are therefore important as a means of avoiding bloodshed and death within the species. The dominant male in any wolf pack stands erect, both tail and head held high, alert to any gestures of challenge from subordinate males. If he must fight to defend his position, he will never kill his antagonist except by accident, for a time comes even in the most ferocious battles when one combatant is clearly the winner. At that point the loser will make an obvious gesture of submission. A wolf will expose his throat, secure in the knowledge that the victor will not bite. Thus the species selects those that are most fit to feed and breed, while at the same time preserving the social unit and keeping a healthy stock in reserve.

Posturings are often accompanied by sound. Dogs and cats are especially vocal; the shrew, as well as being the most ravenous of mammals, is the most vociferous. He seems to be constantly talking, sending out a variety of whispers, squeaks, snarls, and barks as he scampers about in search of prey. Squirrels chatter, woodchucks and marmots whistle, male walruses bellow, and the mating cry of a porcupine is like that of a frightened child. When they howl, wolves close their eyes and shape their lips very carefully. Like the howl of the wolf, the lion's roar may express general self-satisfaction and well-being, for they roar when they are mating, when they have made a kill, or when they are travelling to or from water. In general, sound is used in dense bush areas by members of dispersed species. The polar bear depends on it very little, perhaps because life on the shifting pack ice is always noisy. His ears are small compared with those of his southern relatives.

One of the most striking specializations for sound occurs in a fruit-eating bat of the Congo. The males of this species have enormous larynxes and air-sacs which have so swollen their throats that all other physical activities are subordinated to their ability to make loud sounds. Periodically, they gather for awesome communal roaring sessions.

Marine mammals are excellently adapted to sending and receiving sound. When the beluga whale 'speaks,' it contracts its brow and bulges out the top of its head into a resonating chamber, forcing its signal outward against tremendous water resistance. During a dive, when all parts of the whale's respiratory system may have been collapsed by the extraordinary pressure, the inner ears are automatically kept equalized by air pumped to them as required. The auditory nerves of all cetaceans are larger than those found in other mammals, making them remarkably sensitive to the noises of the sea. Underwater microphones have picked up the calls of finback whales one hundred miles away. Sperm whales communicate over great distances by a variety of clicks, 'muffled smashing sounds,' and grating groans. Other species make similar sounds, as well as sobbings, rusty-hinge creakings, whistles, and rasps like sandpaper on wood. Listeners have described the calls of the humpback whale as 'blats' and 'moos.' So animated are the discussions of dolphins that at times they sound like a whole orchestra tuning up. Clearly, the sea is not a silent place, at least for its cruising mammals.

On land, mammals prefer to rely on smell as the basic communications system. Herbivores such as mice, rabbits, and most ungulates leave persistent and unmistakable trails of scent for carnivores to follow, but at the same time most carnivores have their own strong odours which often forewarn their prey. Among the Mustelids (weasels and skunks) the odours are especially noxious, but these animals are of

The skunk has little need for camouflage; his defence consists of two small glands at the base of his tail which can spray a volatile oil with an acrid odour from as far as twelve feet.

course not the only ones equipped with musk glands. The beaver's ritual depositing of castoreum at chosen spots about his territory is both an assertion of residential rights and a careful attention to etiquette. In this way he keeps up good relations with his neighbours and tells travellers what they need to know. His musk glands are located at the anus, so that scent is deposited with dung, but some ungulates have scent glands between their toes, tunnelling shrews have them on their flanks, and tree-dwelling lemurs have them in their hands.

Many species use message posts on which they leave their musk or urine. Wolves scrupulously maintain a complex communications network with such posts spaced about a mile apart. When he arrives at one, a journeying wolf can tell at once whether the last visitor was young or old, hungry or gorged, male or female. He can also tell the direction of travel and, if she was a female, whether or not she was looking for a mate. Bears also use such posts, reaching up as high as possible to bite and claw at selected trees, thus giving a clear indication of their size. Martens, mink, weasels, and otters all maintain similar musking spots, and in some cases they stand on their front paws while stretching up backward as high as possible to leave their mark. Perhaps those bushes on which rutting stags rub the velvet off new antlers also serve as signal posts, for musk is often left on them from facial glands.

In most species, it is the male who is responsible for routine trail- and boundary-marking.

13 TERRITORIES AND TRADITIONS

Traditions are very important among mammals. What a parent passes on to his or her offspring is a resilient set of responses for behaving correctly in the interests of the group. Social concerns come first, far ahead of individual whims and preferences, and they are constantly being reaffirmed by the maintenance of marking posts, communal dunging places, and traditional singing and meeting spots. Seals and bats

have places of assembly which have been used for centuries, and in some parts of Newfoundland the rocks have been worn down two feet by generations of caribou migrating on exactly the same trails.

The sense of territory varies from species to species, and from season to season. Roaming over hundreds of miles, caribou lack all sense of private property, and each individual shares the largess of the communal range. On the other hand, home ground is so important to a cottontail rabbit that even if it is being run by a dog it will move in a wide circle around its burrow. Experimenters caught one rabbit thirty-five times in two years, always within a circle only 200 yards across. They found that if they carried a rabbit more than three-quarters of a mile away from its den it would be totally lost.

Seals and walruses are all confident travellers, but they keep strict social schedules, meeting at traditional places at appointed times. Northern Hudson Bay is dotted with walrus gathering grounds, and while they are on them, walruses are surpassed only by elephants in displays of herd solidarity. Seal breeding places, or rookeries, are an important device in selection for mating; once a year, these relatively small areas are divided into territories to be won and held by combat among the males. Besides the land, victors win the right to breed, and since the seal is polygamous, several females are fertilized by the dominant types. Landless 'bachelor' bulls are consigned to the edges of the herd.

Among carnivores, territories are often shared and competitors tolerated, provided food supplies are adequate for all, and the social niceties are observed. Message posts are not always purely olfactory. As we have seen, bears bite at their chosen saplings; and cats, raking the bark off trees, both sharpen their claws and leave a calling-card for others in the region. A most important feature of all shared territories is the network of interlocking tracks and trails, some of which are private walks, some of which are highways. Mammals tend to develop a 'kinesthetic' sense which accustoms them

Although walrus herds have been severely thinned by hunting and loss of habitat, the solidarity displayed at their gathering places is still an impressive sight.

to certain pathways, and the habitual use of those trails then permits more concentration on either attack or defence.

For migratory or wandering species, home may be little more than a sheltered spot in which to give birth before travelling on with the herd. For others, homes may range from seasonal residences to well-established villages. Some animals keep summer and winter lodgings; the woodchuck, for example, prefers the open fields in warm weather, but moves into the woods to hibernate. Caves, tree holes, and abandoned burrows all provide ready-made shelters which may be taken as they are or modified to taste. Nests of leaves, grass, or moss are common among hibernators or semi-hibernators. The ferret may line a new burrow with the fur of its former occupants.

The beaver, the muskrat, and the rabbit all have complicated living arrangements. Although a rabbit warren may seem disorganized, it is actually highly segregated, each individual possessing a home range within the communal territory. Itinerant muskrats occasionally share accommodation with a beaver family, but they are themselves highly skilled house-builders. When the time comes for them to settle, they begin by rolling weeds into tiny blocks and packing them among upright stalks.

Aside from man, however, no mammal is a more compulsive architect than the prairie dog, and in no species is the style of dwelling more rigidly a part of social life. Prairie dog towns often contain hundreds of residents and consist of acres of labyrinthine underground passageways. The basic social unit is the coterie – one or two adult males, two or more females, a few juveniles, and several babies. As is the case with the rabbit, each individual has a precise sense of territory, despite the density of the settlement; and he feels compelled to defend that territory if certain bounds of decorum are overstepped. 'Good fences,' as Robert Frost said, 'make good neighbours.' When relatives and friends meet in corridors, they have no difficulty recognizing each other by sight

The caribou is strictly a herd animal. The caribou cow gives birth anywhere on the barrens or the muskeg, and the young, at birth, are strong enough to accompany the herd.

and smell, but they usually confirm identities with a kiss. In fact, they are among the fondest of mammals, constantly kissing, grooming each other, and rubbing necks and noses. Nevertheless, they are susceptible to crowding; when family burrows have become too small, the grandparents or the parents move off to the outskirts of the village and start housekeeping afresh. Their new burrow will have the characteristic storeroom, guardroom, and nest, as well as the carefully mounded entrance, which serves both as a watchtower and as a dike against flash floods. Like their archenemy, the badger, prairie dogs are phenomenal diggers, with strong claws and broad, powerful paws.

14 HARVESTERS AND PREDATORS

For all mammals, whether they are terrestrial, arboreal, or aquatic, the principal concern is to maintain their high metabolism. No matter how successful its defence of home and territory, if the food quest fails the species dies.

The smallest Canadian mammal is also the most voracious. Shrews are mainly insectivores. Each day they must consume their own weight, and despite their diminutive proportions, they will attack mice and even frogs if no other prey can be found. Usually they win battles against much larger foes, for they are the only mammals known to mix poison with their saliva. The poison glands of a single short-tailed shrew are lethal enough to kill 200 mice. Shrews are constantly and gnawingly ravenous; the water shrew has even devised the means to chase down aquatic bugs, scampering across the surface on tiny pontoons of air trapped in its paws.

Both shrews and bats eat their catches immediately, but several other mammals keep larders. These species usually store food throughout the year, although really serious hoard-

Although the black-tailed prairie dogs were probably never overly abundant in Canada, the species is now limited to a reserve in southern Saskatchewan.

67

Chipmunks hoard nuts, which they carry in their cheeks. The coyote (right) *breaks through the snow with his forepaws to catch mice and voles.*

ing only begins with the shortening days of autumn. Chipmunks and deer mice can carry home several days' food in their cheek pouches. Many species of mice keep granaries, and voles and steppe lemmings cut and stack hay. Foxes bury eggs, and moles keep worms captive by snipping off one end of their bodies. Perhaps the most sophisticated preserving techniques, however, are those practised by the red squirrel. Pine cones are its favourite food, and because they will split open and lose their seeds if allowed to dry, the squirrel is always careful to store them in a damp place. This might not be so remarkable if the red squirrel did not also preserve mushrooms by drying them in the sun.

Many large carnivores return to their kills, and bears and cats will sometimes cache carcasses in an attempt to keep them from scavengers. Bears are omnivorous, feeding on game, insects, honey, berries, and vegetation; grizzlies, in fact, are interested in almost everything except human flesh. Voyaging on ice-floes, polar bears probably travel farthest on the hunt – often 1,000 miles – and will swim fifteen miles to reach icebergs where seals have congregated. Their stalking of seals, either on icebergs or on the pack ice, is long and cautious. As he approaches, a polar bear will move in the shade wherever possible, and he will hide his black nose behind a paw or a piece of snow.

Among cats, the killing technique is to strike at the neck, severing the spinal cord and causing almost instantaneous death. If the neck is very long, the cat will bite twice – once just ahead of the shoulders and once at the base of the skull. Wolves kill less decisively, avoiding hooves and biting wherever they can.

Many predators have learned to take advantage of their prey's curiosity. A common trick among Chipewyan Indians was to draw a caribou from the herd by clinging together one behind the other and walking in lock step, coaxing the animal on until it could be killed from ambush. Deer are intensely curious about anything that moves, and they will often allow hunters to approach very close. Foxes are masters of a decoy

The badger (left) *is well equipped with teeth and claws. His prey is a bull snake. Many bears,* like this brown bear, *find man to be a ready supplier of food.*

activity called 'tolling.' A fox, ever watchful, will toss and play with a stick until the duck, which is the real object of his attentions, has moved close enough to be seized.

Like the polar bear's, the fox's diet varies with the seasons. He is a great opportunist who will take what chance provides, but his daily summer diet usually consists of about a pound of woodchuck meat, mice, or wild flowers. In autumn he shifts his attention to insects, particularly crickets and grasshoppers, and in winter he relies on cottontails for about 60 per cent of his needs. The remainder consists of leftovers from wolf kills, and of mice and voles, which foxes can catch through a five-inch cover of snow.

For all Canadian mammals winter is the leanest time. Some sleep through it, some migrate, and some simply endure. Not even wolves can hunt in snow deeper than sixteen inches, and deer and moose 'yard up' as the snow accumulates, stamping down large areas and stripping surrounding trees of all edible buds and twigs. Their demands are considerable; a single moose will eat forty to fifty pounds of twigs per day. In the autumn, muskoxen eat continuously, storing up huge fat reserves against the coming famine. They endure winter, moving as little as possible, facing away from the wind, waiting until the snow softens and they can once again dig down to the tundra herbage.

As a ruminant, the muskox has special digestive equipment which smaller herbivores do not possess. Squirrels, rabbits, beavers, and prairie dogs share the problem of breaking down the high percentage of cellulose in their regular diets. Cellulose is difficult to digest, and the intestines of these animals are unequipped to deal with it in one passage; consequently, they eat their food twice, consuming their own feces in a nocturnal activity called *coprophagy*. The first run-through produces a greenish pellet which is eaten just as it is voided; the second produces the familiar dark dung.

Hooves, claws, and teeth – most mammals carry with them all the eating utensils they require. As a tool-user, the sea

69

The formation and structure of teeth and jaws greatly aids mammals in their survival. The teeth of the wolf, deer, porcupine, and primate are well suited to their diets.

otter is a member of a small and exceptional group that includes man. Sea otters are very fond of molluscs, and they may sometimes be seen floating contentedly beyond the surf, cracking shellfish on a rock perched on their stomachs. Clams are also a staple in the walrus diet, but walruses use their tusks to prod them from the bottom mud, sometimes 200 to 300 feet below the surface of the water. In one day, an earnest walrus may suck 3,000 clams from their shells. For a walrus to seek larger prey is unusual, but occasionally – perhaps because of deformity or age – a walrus turns to seal killing. Swimming on his back, he glides beneath his victim, waiting for it to raise its head to breathe. At that moment, when the seal is most vulnerable, he seizes it with his flippers and strikes with his tusks.

Narwhals, beluga whales, bottlenose whales, porpoises, and dolphins all eat fish. Killer whales use their slightly protuberant teeth on the larger creatures of the sea, and the great sperm whale dines on octopi and squid. But the largest mammals feed on some of the smallest creatures. Baleen whales, such as the blue, the fin, and the right, may grow to weigh 150 tons and to stretch over a hundred feet. Their entire rear third is an enormous engine of muscle capable of developing more than 500 horsepower, and their forward third is all head and massive mouth. Hanging inside their mouths are curtains of baleen – that same whalebone that braced the corsets of Victorian matrons. Its natural function is to act as a filter, straining drifting planktonic organisms from the water so that they may then, in their millions, be licked down the gullet. Because plankton is richest near the surface in polar regions, this is where baleen whales are most often found, browsing like the regal harvesters they are. As breeding seasons approach, however, they move towards warmer latitudes, there to begin the graceful courtship rituals which caused D. H. Lawrence to write:

They say the sea is cold, but the sea contains
The hottest blood of all, and the wildest, the most urgent.

15 SELECTIVE BREEDING

Good poker players watch their opponents' eyes. Would-be seducers watch the girl's eyes. Both know that, even if body movements are carefully suppressed, eyes send an involuntary and infallible signal: at pleasant sights, the pupils dilate. When she is receptive, a girl's eyes always appear larger and softer, making her whole face more attractive. Such visual signals are more important for man than either sound or smell; indeed, he has evolved a whole repertory of gestures to indicate sexual availability.

Only man breeds incessantly. Other animals are restricted to certain seasons of the year determined by several factors, including light and temperature, timed to produce young when conditions are most favourable for their survival. In each pairing, what is involved is not just the final male-female relationship but the whole social organization. Mating consists of three stages: selection, courtship, and copulation.

Competition among males is the usual selective device. In no species but man does this competition become a fight to the death. Accidents do occur, of course – the antlers of rutting stags become locked, and beaten wolves will sometimes die of wounds – but the natural tendency is for effective selection with minimal damage. In some cases, selection is made with no physical contact at all. The male Congolese bats with the mighty vocal organs gather both to assess population requirements and to establish – peacefully but with tremendous din – which should breed. In their case, voice is a secondary sexual characteristic like the narwhal's tusk, the buck's antlers, the hooded seal's inflatable forehead, the killer whale's enlarged flippers and fin, and the male human's beard. All are related to potency and thus function as selective devices; a eunuch has no beard, and if a buck suffers testicular damage, his antlers will be stunted or misshapen. In the wild, such individuals stand little chance of securing a place in the breeding hierarchy.

Other species besides the fruit bats establish their hierarchies through formalized competition. Male coyotes regularly gather to sing in traditional 'choir lofts.' March hares are not really mad, despite all the leaping, boxing, kicking, and follow-the-leader that goes on among them. Before rut begins, elks also dance, and many male ungulates roar, play pushing and wrestling games, and engage in various forms of stylized display. They are determining who is fit to mate and, if the species is polygamous, how many mates each dominant male should have.

Polygamy is usual among gregarious species. Seals and sea lions secure harems of fifteen to forty females. Sperm whales are also polygamous, but baleen whales are monog-amous – a condition that, among land animals, is associated with especially keen territoriality. The walrus, the moose, the fox, the wolf, and the beaver all prefer monogamy, although not all mate for life. Small rodents, on the other hand, are almost completely promiscuous.

At certain times of the year, the females of most mammal-ian species undergo a period of *oestrus*, or 'heat.' Duration and frequency of these periods vary greatly; seals and weasels have only one oestrus cycle per year, but rodents have re-peated periods through extended breeding seasons. During oestrus the female emits olfactory and behaviourial stimuli that announce her approaching readiness to conceive and which make her irresistible to the male. Oestrus attracts the male before ovulation, so that he will be in attendance during the critical hours. Male deer and rodents have periods of rut which correspond to the females' oestrus and make doubly sure that fertilization will occur.

Even within a species, courtship behaviour is never con-stant, although it usually includes a variety of kisses, caresses, and bites. Seals and sea lions rub necks. Whales hurl them-selves exuberantly out of the water. Walruses hold a com-munal male dance before the females, displaying their strength and adornments. Platypuses chase each other in circles. Squirrels invent seductive demonstrations with their tails, and as they approach the female, they make whimpering baby sounds to arouse her maternal instinct and weaken any resis-

The polygamous bull elk will defend his herd of cows with great ferocity. In order to take a harem from another bull, the threatening male must almost kill his opponent.

Camouflage — safety of the young

Although both the cottontail rabbit (right) *and the white-tailed deer* (above) *are preyed upon by other animals, they have taken different paths to ensure the protection of their young.*

The young of the cottontail are blind. After birth they are placed in a depression in the ground for their protection. As they are small and blend in well with their surroundings, they are protected against predators. As a species, rabbits are aided by their prolific reproduction. Three or four litters of four to seven young are born each year. Thus the species is assured that some rabbits will survive to replace their parents, for only a few rabbits reach maturity each year.

Deer, on the other hand, give birth only once a year to one or two fawns. The fawn above is only three hours old, but is already capable of standing. When the doe goes in search of food, the fawn will remain motionless, its spots providing a perfect camouflage against the sun-dappled earth. Even from close range, it gives no sign of its existence. It emits no sound and has no odour. The mother leaves it unattended for long periods so predators will not be attracted to the spot by her scent. By fall, the fawn's spots will be gone. Then the deer will have only its keen senses to protect it from predators.

tance she may yet have. This device is also used by courting hamsters, field mice, and some dogs. In many species, the male places his neck over the female's as a test of her receptivity and as a prelude to actual copulation.

Porcupines, according to an old woodsmen's joke, mate carefully. Their position, however, is no different from that assumed by most other mammals – the male mounts the female from behind, forelegs holding her back and sides. Beavers mate face-to-face, sitting up. Whales leave the water altogether, their bellies joined. Primates use a variety of positions, and orangutans especially are great sexual gymnasts. Bats copulate hanging upside down, but the male remains conventionally behind the female. One of the oddest mating habits is that developed by the female rat, who takes a vicious snap at the male's head as he dismounts; rat lovemaking therefore tends to end in an athletic backward leap.

Quick copulation is practised by the hunted, not by the hunters. Dogs, bears, martens, and related species remain joined for fairly long intervals because their penises are equipped with erectile nodes which swell immediately after ejaculation, completely filling the vagina and preventing the escape of semen. Longest herbivore copulation – about half an hour – is that of the armoured rhinoceros. The *Dasycercus*, a marsupial mouse of lizard-like disposition, is said to embrace for twenty-four hours at a time, but most rodents remain together only for seconds, although they may meet often. During oestrus, a female rat will copulate 300 or 400 times with as many as half a dozen males. On the other hand, a prime enemy of the rat, the ferret, will sometimes remain three hours in a single act of mating. Individual lion copulations may be comparatively brief, although repeated frequently over a few hours. Like most carnivores, the lion has a strong inhibition against biting the female, but at the moment of ejaculation his jaws will close on the back of her neck. A wolf will make the same gesture, as will a bear.

After mating, male and female may never meet again. The vital act has been performed, and the embryo crucial to the

The lynx, with its heavy coat and broad furred feet, is well suited to the Canadian climate. The young are helpless at birth and remain with their mother about six months.

continuation of the species has begun its long journey – a journey regulated by rhythms of which the mother's body is a part. In most cases, birth will occur within a predictable number of weeks or months; occasionally however, particularly in northern climates where food cycles can fluctuate erratically, conception may have occurred at an awkward time. When this happens, some bears, deer, and martens can simply suspend their pregnancies. The process is called delayed implantation. When this occurs, the ovum is arrested in its development and kept dormant for weeks or months before normal pregnancy is resumed.

With very few exceptions, mammalian parenthood requires a period of child care and training longer than the pregnancy itself. Unless she is a member of a gregarious herding species, or unless she mates for life, this responsibility falls completely on the mother. She must feed, guard, clean, warm, and teach

16 PARENTAL PROTECTION

Young monotremes grow inside their eggs, and marsupials enjoy the extended protection of their mother's pouch. Placental young, however, must either be born sufficiently developed to move and keep warm, or be protected in some refuge while they mature. Caribou have favoured calving areas where the herd pauses while gravid females move to its edges. But these periods of rest are short; when the herd pushes on, the young must follow. In contrast, expectant polar bears stop travelling altogether for two or three months. In November or December, the mother polar bear gives birth in a comfortable den hollowed out about ten feet under the surface of the snow. The warmth of her breath and body will have lined its inside with insulating ice, and the temperature there may be forty degrees higher than on the surface. For many weeks she can support her babies and herself on her personal stores of fat.

In general, the young of burrowing species are born comparatively helpless. They are usually blind and deaf, and their lack of hair makes them especially dependent on their

Life on top of the world

The mountain goat is protected by its daring and agility. It is capable of negotiating a cliff using ridges no more than two inches wide as footholds. The hooves of the mountain goat provide the animal with much of its stability. Under the hooves are concave hollows, which act like suction cups when weight is pressed on them.

The kid, usually one each year, is born on a high ridge. Within days, it must follow its mother on the seemingly impassable mountain trails in search of food.

An adult mountain goat is capable of executing leaps of twelve feet across forbidding chasms. The survival of the young depends on its ability to remain with its mother and to negotiate such startling leaps as this one.

Young goat kids are also protected by a slightly darker lacing of brown hairs on the back, which camouflage them from the golden eagle, their greatest enemy. From the air the eagle sees only the adult goats, who have nothing to fear from this predator.

In the winter, a herd of mountain goats will select a sheltered spot, usually halfway up the mountain. At this height they are protected from their enemies, but not from the biting cold and stinging wind that blows from the north. In this season the animals have only their thick coats and their great agility to protect them from the freezing air and the danger of avalanches.

78

mother's body. They mature relatively quickly, however; if they are field mice, they may be having children of their own within six weeks. Swift maturation and remarkable fecundity (a female may have 130 young per year) make mice an important food source for many predators. They survive, like rabbits, through sheer weight of numbers. Short life and rapid turnover of generations give a species the advantage of frequent gene combinations and, hence, greater adaptability; but they tend to go with small size and unstable populations. Long life and long dependency, on the other hand, are usually associated with large ranges, more stable environments, and fewer young.

Most mammals are born head first, but porpoises arrive tail first and immediately swim to the surface for their first breath of air. Newborn manatees are less alert, and need to be buoyed up on their mother's body. Many marine mammals are equipped to help their young with the difficult problem of simultaneous suckling and breathing. Special muscles contract their udders and squirt the milk down their baby's throat.

On land, mothers grow especially attentive of their own hind ends just before giving birth. Hormonal changes have begun to ensure that the newborn young will be licked clean and their breathing stimulated. Both wanderers and nest builders eat their placenta as soon as it emerges – part of a general cleanup which helps to foil predators. Also, the placenta contains hormones which may help to begin the flow of milk.

The food hunt may take new mothers from their nest, but never far, and never for long. As soon as possible, the young venture forth with their mother, often trailing behind in squeaking caravans. They learn by watching her, by imitating, and by playing; the most playful species are also the most intelligent. The first law for any mammal with young is *never lose contact*. Strange noises cause cow moose to look towards

This donkey, only twenty minutes old, is encouraged to stand. The care given by the mother immediately after birth is essential to the survival of all mammals. Instinctively, she will lick the infant and ensure that it is breathing.

their calves. The ferocity of ordinarily timid creatures in protecting their young is legendary. One of the most profitable tricks of hunters was to find a baby walrus and beat it until it cried. Because walruses are exceptionally protective, not only the mother but all adults within hearing would race to the youngster's aid – and to their own destruction.

17 EDGE OF EXTINCTION

Tusks and teeth, hooves, horns, and claws – these are the weapons evolution has provided. Sometimes they are used for attack, sometimes for defence. If conditions do not change too swiftly, these weapons are sufficient to allow each species to maintain its ecological position; they are factors in the correct functioning of the whole. Any ecosystem operates as it does because its creatures are what they are, and vice versa. Normally, the hurt and terrified baby walrus would be well protected both by the herd instinct and by the great tusks of its older relatives. Even a polar bear will flee an enraged walrus. But the carefully evolved protective mechanisms of the walrus are the very things that work against it when it encounters the cunning and greed of man. To the sailors on wooden ships, walrus hide was a source of durable rigging, and to them and their descendants the two-foot tusks brought a handsome price in the ivory markets of the world. As a result, the once extensive herds have dwindled to a few scattered colonies. Like the muskox, whose superb circular defence was impregnable to all natural enemies, the walrus has no protection against a long-range bullet.

Happy chance for many years saved most baleen whales from the harpooner's gun. With the exception of the right whale – which was called 'right' because its carcass floated – all baleen whales sank when shot. Then, in a triumph of technology, Norwegian engineers invented the means to inflate whales' corpses and keep them afloat until the factory ship arrived. In the century since that invention, the greatest mammals that ever lived have been brought to the edge of extinction; indeed, some may already have passed over, for

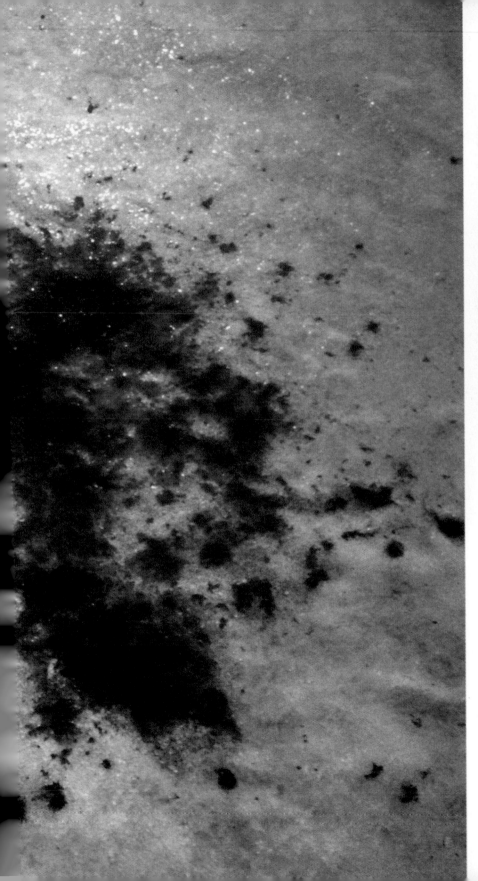

Slaughter of the young

The outrage resulting from worldwide attention to methods of killing harp seals has caused conservation measures to be enacted for their preservation. The white fur of these young seals has been eagerly sought by southern markets, and as a result, this abundant mammal is in danger of serious depletion.

Seals are awkward creatures on land, having only their front flippers to aid in propulsion. The infants are particularly vulnerable, however. They are born on land or ice floes, and must learn to swim later.

Although they are only one of the many animals that are helpless against man's weapons and greed, these seals have attracted particular attention. Harmless to man, they have posed no threat to justify their near extinction.

83

the mating calls of the blue whale, the fin, and the humpback often go unanswered.

Few predators will kill for trivial reasons. The wolverine, which shares with the cape buffalo the reputation for being the most vicious and cunning of mammals, will apparently sometimes kill quite casually, and the fox will kill shrews, moles, and weasels, although (perhaps because of their musky odour) they are not part of his diet. Although primitive man may sometimes kill for decorative or ceremonial purposes, in general he makes full use of his prey, eating the flesh, carving implements from the bones, and stitching the hides into clothing, tents, and boats. The hunting motives of civilized man, however, are far less easy to explain, for whim and fashion have played major roles. Rare furbearers are trapped so that rich women may have coats and stoles. Infant harp seals die on the ice so that their fur may become boots and coin purses. Millions of bison were slaughtered, and their awesome herds were swept away forever, not because the hides were needed or because their meat was put to good use, but because buffalo tongue had become a delicacy in eastern restaurants. Polar bear rugs still command a high black-market price despite the fact that the bear is protected under law. Until recently the white rhinoceros was poached relentlessly because of an oriental belief that its powdered horn was an aphrodisiac. Every year hundreds of thousands of prairie dogs, woodchucks, and other small creatures die in order to satisfy the dubious needs of marksmen.

No matter how perfect the personal armament of these animals, no matter how subtle their protective colorations or warning systems, to modern man they are pathetically vulnerable. If they escape our wiles and weapons, they fall victim to our greed and ignorance, for in our search for resources we often destroy habitats unthinkingly. Fewer pine trees mean fewer porcupines, and fewer porcupines mean fewer fishers. Just as no animal has ever survived the loss of its skin, none has inborn defences against the stripping of its habitat.

WAYLAND DREW

Muskox form a circle as protection from their enemies.

PART FOUR
ADAPTATIONS FOR SURVIVAL

Everybody knows what is meant if someone is described as adaptable. It means that they fit easily into changing circumstances, or do many different things equally well. We use adapters on cameras and water pipes so that dissimilar things may work smoothly together. But the verb 'to adapt' has itself adapted to a somewhat different meaning in the language of biology. To a biologist any characteristic of an organism that improves its chances of survival, and especially of reproduction, is an adaptation. Adaptations are arrived at by natural selection. Any change in function or structure that allows the organism to increase and multiply will be found more and more frequently in each generation. When these favourable characteristics have become established throughout the species as adaptations, the evolution of the organism has advanced. This seems clear enough, and while there is abundant evidence of the importance of adaptations in the

This muskrat is an albino. This recessive characteristic appears in many animals, but because it does not provide the individual with long-term advantages, it does not become widely established.

progress of evolution, nevertheless there is by no means a clear concensus on the when, where, why, and how of adaptive changes.

Mammals are not outstanding examples of the infinite variety of adjustments whereby each organism fits itself into the niche it occupies in the living world. Compared with insects, for example, the adaptations of mammals often seem gross and simple. Mammals are, however, more flexible in their response to external influences. It has been suggested that the evolution of the brain is the most important single factor in the adaptation of vertebrates, of which mammals are the dominant class. The so-called 'lower orders' depend entirely on blind instinct and, if they are to survive at all, must be totally adapted to an inflexible program.

The cold-blooded vertebrates – reptiles, amphibians, and fishes – are unable to adapt to extremes of temperature and in winter must find some place where they will be protected from freezing. A few of the mammals achieve the same end by hibernating, but most of them share a few physiological adjustments sufficient to see them through. These include seasonal changes in metabolism to produce more fat for

87

insulation or to provide body heat and energy; the growing of more and longer hair, and sometimes a different kind of hair; seasonal changes of colour on those species that turn white in winter; and finally the shedding of winter hair and the absorption of excess fat with the return of weather more compatible with their normal body temperatures. These are fundamental or minimal adjustments to the climate of the north temperate zone, which varies through the year from tropic heat to Arctic cold. Most of our mammals depend on nothing beyond these minimal changes. Their basic adaptation for coping with a difficult climate is the ability to withstand real hardship for several months each year.

A look at two well-known species and their difficulties might suggest how close to the line many of our comparatively non-specialized mammals live. The white-tailed deer was ideally equipped to live in the moderate part of the temperate zone, as far north as the Great Lakes. But as lumbering, agriculture, and uncontrolled forest fires destroyed the original mature forest during the last century, deer surged out of their original range, pushing up even into the edge of the boreal zone. As a prolific species occupying a hitherto unexploited range, the deer managed to survive for many years in spite of snow depths for which they were poorly adapted and which often brought them to the edge of disaster in bad winters. In recent years, with a deteriorating food supply because of natural forest succession, too-efficient fire control, and excessive hunting pressure, the climate seems to be winning the battle, and deer have suffered a drastic reduction in numbers, although they still flourish on their original range wherever there is sufficient cover.

An interesting comparision is found in the raccoon, also a forest animal of southern origin that followed man as he pushed north in search of new country. The 'coon is not a hibernator, but is close enough to the bear family to have instincts in that direction, and north of the 45th parallel most of them 'den up' for the worst part of the winter. They make a poor job of it, however, emerging in February, in perhaps

As a growing lumbering industry cleared the forests in many northern areas, thereby encouraging second growth, many white-tailed deer surged into this new habitat.

three or four feet of snow. At such times, it is impossible for them to find food except from human sources, and many are lost. Unlike the deer, which needs forest for both cover and food, the 'coon shows a greater adaptability by changing its habitat completely and literally moving in with man, sheltering in his barns and other outbuildings and eating his garbage. Often 'coons subsist and even raise young within the limits of cities and towns.

18 NORTHERN MODIFICATIONS

Adaptation is not a tidy subject. It would almost seem that the winters of the temperate zone, although often severe, are just not long enough for natural selection to establish effective winter protection. However, if we go a few hundred miles further north and beyond, into the heart of the boreal zone, we find such mammals as the polar bear and the moose, which have effectively adapted to winter.

The polar bear has been adapted over eons of time for life in polar seas. Long, waterproof hair, white to match its surroundings; a long neck, always useful for a swimmer; non-skid hair on the soles of its feet for walking on ice: all make it possible for the polar bear to live and thrive in conditions that would be fatal to wholly terrestrial bears such as the black and the grizzly.

A moose in its natural setting, browsing twigs and small branches or plunging its head into a lake to pull up water plants, does not appear to be specially suited to its activities. Everything about a moose suggests awkwardness and a lack of finesse. It pulls down small trees and crudely breaks off their branches; plunges its head in the water with a movement as artistic as dropping a bucket into a well; charges out of the water when alarmed with the smoothness of a tank crossing

In early spring, the raccoon is faced with such uncertainties as recently thawed ice and an irregular food supply. This raccoon tests the thin ice before retreating.

91

a river; and crashes off through the forest like a bulldozer, carrying a fifty-pound pair of antlers on its head. As a symbol of untamed strength and disregard for petty obstacles it is magnificent, and as a source of speculative adaptations it is a storehouse.

Parts of the anatomy that are visibly specialized are generally assumed to have adaptive value. The moose has a ridiculously long nose, extending far out beyond its mouth, a 'bell' of long hair hanging beneath its chin, and a tail so small that it has to be looked for to be seen. Unless they are functional we would not expect such features to become established by natural selection, but no function has been recorded for any of these. The long legs that elevate the moose to a height of close to seven feet have been thought of as adaptations related to moving through deep snow, wading in water, reaching food plants far above the ground, and running to escape from its only predator, the wolf. Undoubtedly they are useful for all these things, but they also prevent the moose, which has a short neck, from reaching grass or other low forage without getting down on its knees. Long legs are both an advantage and a hazard among the marshy lakes and beaver ponds of moose country, and here one visible adaptation is noticeable. When crossing a swamp clogged by moss-covered logs and buried glacial stones, the legs are conspicuously lifted straight up until the foot has cleared the surface before it is advanced. This is surely an adaptation to prevent broken legs, and well illustrates the functioning of natural selection, which would soon remove from the population those moose with a propensity for breaking their legs.

At first glance the phenomenon of animals that change from some darker colour to white in winter seems the perfect example of adaptation to the environment. A white animal against white snow does not attract the eye and is thus protected from detection by its enemies. There is, however, no direct material evidence to prove that a white covering in winter acts as an effective camouflage to protect its owner

Unlike many mammals, including the moose, the polar bear seems to adapt well to captivity. This one, in Stanley Park, Vancouver, seems to enjoy its new environment.

92

Ungainly magnificence

The moose is the world's largest living deer, standing five and a half to six feet at the shoulders. It has a long face with an overhanging muzzle and disproportionately long legs. It is an excellent swimmer, spending more time than most deer in the water. Its long legs enable it to wade in fairly deep water for aquatic plants which compose a large part of its diet during spring and summer months. Occasionally, it will completely submerge itself to obtain aquatic plants.

Moose are solitary animals, living usually only in family groups. Several moose may feed in the same area, but they tend to move about independentally and return to their solitary existence after feeding. Their basic diet consists of broad-leafed trees and shrubs supplemented by aquatic plants and, in winter, by balsam fir and bark peeled from trees.

Calves weigh twenty-five to thirty-five pounds at birth (usually late May or early June) and grow at an incredible rate. They may reach a weight of 400 to 600 pounds in one year.

Because of its long legs, the young moose (above) must kneel to use the natural salt lick. Although a disadvantage for grazing, the long legs enable a full-grown moose to browse trees growing nine feet from the ground.

95

from predation. Those animals that stay white all year, such as the polar bear and the Arctic wolf, may be seen for miles during snowless periods, and the familiar varying hare, one of the most preyed on of all mammals at all seasons, turns white in the fall whether or not the ground is snow-covered. In the southern part of its range, where snow is rare in the fall, the mortality of hares is greatly increased, as anyone who has hunted hares at that season can testify.

The lemming, a large mouse of the Arctic tundra, constitutes a large part of the food supply of many carnivorous birds and mammals of that region. The brown lemming and collared lemming occupy much of the same range, but the latter turns white in winter while the former does not. The conspicuous red fox lives side by side with the white Arctic fox in the northern taiga. The mink and the long-tailed weasel occupy the same range across southern Canada, and apart from the fact that the mink is somewhat the larger, they are quite similar in appearance and habits. The weasel turns white in winter, but the mink remains dark brown or black at all seasons. Thus, the instant assumption that colour changes are an adaptation may be too easy an answer. It seems certain these changes have something to do with snow and Arctic conditions generally, but the haphazard manner in which they now occur suggests the possibility that they could be left-over from some earlier era, when their use was more direct and general.

19 INTERLOCKING CLUSTERS

Surely the test of an animal's adjustment to its surroundings is the extent to which it is able to carry on its normal activities throughout the year. Which is the better adaptation: the bear that avoids confrontation with the hungry months of winter by hibernating, or the wolf that increases its hunting efforts and depends on industry and endurance to maintain itself? I would suggest the bear, which changes its way of life completely to conform with changes in its environment. The wolf's only concession to the hard times of winter is to grow

Adaptive coloration

Although it is uncertain what advantages are gained by seasonal changes in coloration, many animals have distinct summer and winter coats. The summer coat of the Arctic hare (above) *seems to provide camouflage. Only its tail and the tips of its ears maintain their winter colours. In some parts of its range, this species is white all year round. Found only in the most northern regions of Canada, it is truly an Arctic animal. Its large feet enable it to hop about on the top of the snow.*

The long-tailed weasel is found only in southern Canada and in the United States and Mexico. Shown here (right) *in its winter coat, it also provides an interesting example in effective coloration. In nearly all of Canada, this seasonal colour change takes place yearly, but further south weasels remain brown throughout the year. Weasels are extremely efficient mousers, although they often also raid hen houses. They remain active throughout the year and are extremely high-strung creatures with a very high metabolism rate.*

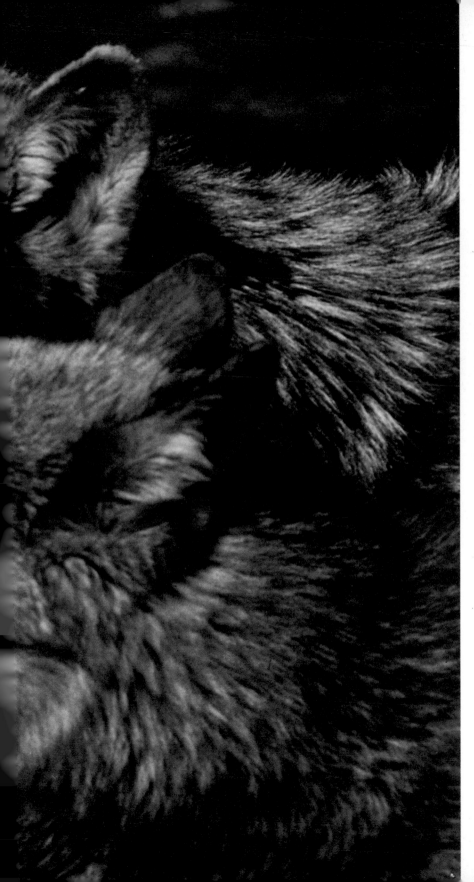

a layer of dense underfur to help conserve its body heat. This is an automatic physiological change over which the wolf has no control, quite a different thing from preparing a den or storing food.

The hibernation of the bear differs considerably from that of the woodchuck, although both prepare a den and retire into it before winter sets in. Whereas the bear never becomes truly dormant, is easily awakened, and the females even have their young and care for them during this period, the woodchuck sinks into a deep lethargy in which it is completely unconscious, and over which it has as little control as the wolf has of its underfur. And there are still other hibernators among the ground squirrels that go the bear one better and lay in an ample supply of food. Thus, they do not need to carry excess fat when they retire and are well provided for in early spring before the usual food sources are available. Thrift in these squirrels would readily become established through natural selection, which would certainly favour those that tended to store food over those that did not.

A wolf has long legs and big feet, and by the nature of things this equipment must be helpful to an animal running in snow. A deer has even longer legs, but small feet, and if the snow is not deeper than the length of its legs the greater length might balance any advantage the wolf has in its big feet. But the average deer is heavier than the average wolf, so the wolf might still have an advantage except that the deer's running gait consists of a series of high jumps, so that its body clears the snow by several feet between jumps. Then it brings its feet together and lands them in an area not more than a foot in diameter. The wolf does not have a similar bounding gait, but runs with its body comparatively close to the snow. Since it does not bunch its feet, the footprints are separate, often close to two feet apart. A galloping wolf in slow motion would resemble a travelling 'inch-worm,' and at high speed suggests the rapid flexing of a steel spring. It does not cover as much ground as a deer at each jump, but jumps

The much-maligned wolf provides a vital link in the interlocking adaptations of Canada's wildlife. A sociable animal, wolves live in packs and often hunt in relays.

faster. It is, in fact, a sprinter, which explains why it has difficulty bringing down a deer in the bush but overhauls one quickly on the hard-packed snow of a frozen lake. The preferred gait of a wolf in deep, soft snow is a walk, with the pack moving in a single file. If the snow is deep enough to seriously impede deer, it is next to impossible for wolves. They can only follow in the deer's trail and harry it from behind until it makes the mistake of running out on a lake. In summer, a deer instinctively tries to reach water, as it is an excellent swimmer and wolves do not like to swim. If a deer stays in the bush in deep snow it can and often does discourage wolves, who often give up within a mile, but it may be frustrated by obstacles, especially quick drop-offs, snow-plowed roads, or brush piles. The deer's greatest handicap, however, is its tendency to depend on open water for safety; frozen water is its downfall.

There are few better examples of the interlocking adaptations of predator and prey than this one of deer and wolves; a whole cluster of adaptations on each side, the advantage shifting back and forth and just balancing out in the long run. A chase begins like a throw of dice, with the ability of the pursuer to overtake staked against the ability of the pursued to escape, ensuring that the hunter will take enough but not too much, and the prey will escape but not too often. Thus they work out a population balance for both – they are adapted to each other.

20 ADAPTATIONS TO HABITAT

Another realistic view of mammalian adaptations in action is provided by the thirty-odd species of marine mammals, about one-quarter of the total list, which inhabit Canada's coastal waters for at least part of the year. The whales, includ-

A mule deer fawn assumes a frozen stance with its head on the ground. This instinctive response to danger aids in its survival, for in this position it is virtually invisible.

ing porpoises and dolphins, are the farthest removed in appearance from the popular conception of a mammal, but they have all the mammalian parts in modified form, and nothing, except their way of life, to link them with fishes. Although there is no doubt whatever that they are true mammals, traces of hind limbs still to be found in some species form the only visible link with the past. Their adaptation to a different medium is complete and seems even more perfect than that of the mammals living on dry land.

Seals, which are more closely tied to the land than whales, show other signs of their terrestrial origin, but they are entirely dependent on the sea for food. Although all four legs have been modified to swimming flippers, the feet still have toes with nails. In true, or hair seals, the legs have no function and simply trail behind, but in the sea lions, or fur seals, and the walrus, they are used for propulsion. Whales and the walrus no longer have a body covering of hair and have no external ears, but fur seals have both. Hair seals have lost their ears and retained their body hair, but as there is no underfur, the hair has little insulating value, and body heat is retained by a layer of blubber under the skin. It seems rather obvious that natural selection still has work to do in this group.

Perhaps some of the adaptations that have come about will undergo additional change. The two great ivory tusks of the walrus are not offensive weapons, although said to be used in defence. Mostly they are used to dig for shell-fish, and one wonders whether such cumbersome equipment is really necessary for this task. As for the narwhal, the original unicorn, its single tusk, as far as anybody knows, is not used for any practical purpose.

Whales have modified many of the mammalian characteristics for a life in the sea. Their forelimbs have become stabilizers and their hind limbs have completely disappeared. They propel themselves by an up-and-down motion of their horizontal flukes. Hair is replaced by an insulating layer of fat as a protective covering. Whales have small ears and little or no sense of smell. Their nostrils, originally at the end of their snout, are now on the top of their head.

103

Between land and sea

The general direction of evolution has been from the sea to land; occasionally, however, the direction has reversed. Somewhere in the evolutionary history of the seal, adaptations occurred that provided for survival in the sea. Seals may have first ventured to the water in search of food or to escape their enemies. Now they are linked to both land and sea.

Seals are divided into two groups: the true seals (leopard, ribbon, and elephant seals) and eared seals (sea lions and fur seals). True seals are more adapted to aquatic life. Their hind flippers are joined to form a tail and they lack external ears.

Sea lions (shown here) *have retained external ears and are capable of rotating their hind flippers forward to aid in locomotion on land. The body can be supported by the flippers, front and back, on which they can 'walk'. In the water, the limbs project backwards and form effective paddles.*

The sea lion is thus balanced between land and sea. It looks to the sea for its food: lamprey, squid, sand lance, pollack, and other fish. But it returns to the land to rest and to breed.

Male sea lions gather harems of ten to twenty females each year on rocky islets. Here each female gives birth to one pup, which she suckles for at least three months. Although the young can swim at birth, as a rule they remain on land for several weeks before they take to the water.

The sea lions here were photographed off the coast of Long Beach on Vancouver Island. They can be found all along the west coast, sunning on the rocky islets and shores from California to British Columbia and the Bering Sea. Although they will occasionally venture into the larger river systems, they tend to congregate along the shores. Only during migration do they take to the water for long distances.

It may be only a coincidence that some of the more striking adaptations among inland mammals are found in semi-aquatic species. The river otter, for example, is better adapted to a year-round life in the temperate zone than any other mammal. With a cylindrical, streamlined body covered by short, dense fur, very short ears, tail tapering to a point, and webs between the toes of all four feet, it is the perfect amphibian, slipping through the water like an eel but perfectly at home on land, where its low-slung body and short, strong legs allow it to negotiate every kind of forest cover with equal ease. When there is snow on the ground, it uses its body as a ski, sliding down all grades. On the level, it proceeds by a series of bounds followed by a slide, like a child running and sliding on a frozen pond. All through the winter it follows the same routes, uses the same waters, and eats the same foods as in summer, for it moves under snow or ice as easily as on the surface. Some foods may be even more available; hibernating frogs need only to be picked up rather than caught, and muskrats hiding in lodges or bank burrows are easier to catch than when swimming free in a marsh. It is also more convenient to dive through a hole in the ice in the middle of a beaver pond than to swim all over the pond looking for prey. Comparing an otter rolling about on snow-covered ice, playing with a fish or frog that it has just brought up through icy water from the muddy depths, with a carefree otter family chasing each other in the warm waters of summer, certainly suggests the ultimate in adaptation to a sharply variable climate.

The beaver, occupying the same general habitat as the otter, presents an interesting comparison in adaptive behaviour. The two animals' structural adaptations to an aquatic habitat are of similar magnitude but differently distributed. The beaver has only its hind feet webbed, but has a broad, paddle-like tail which the otter lacks. Because the beaver's life-style does not call for speed, it is short and plump rather than long and slender, and thus has greater

The pond formed by a beaver dam provides the beaver with protection and security. It also serves as ready access to trees and encourages the growth of aquatic plants.

106

The carefree otter

The otter is a carefree, happy creature, equally at ease in the water and on land. It adapts well to a variety of conditions, including captivity. The otter (above), *photographed in Stanley Park, Vancouver, seems content enough as he floats on his back.*

The otter is capable of swimming underwater for a quarter of a mile and speeding after fish faster than they can swim. Fish are the otter's favourite food. It catches them with its sharp canine teeth and swallows them head first, so that the sharp bones will pass harmlessly through its bowels.

Exceedingly playful animals, otters will spend hours sliding down a mud bank or tobogganing on the snow on their bellies. In winter they are protected by their short thick fur, which is overlaid with long guard hairs, and by a layer of fat which covers the entire body.

Otters have a highly developed sense of direction. A pair of otters taken from Victoria Harbour to Stanley Park later escaped and were able to find their way 'home' over a distance of at least seventy miles, about fifteen of which were over water.

109

Roadside sights

Although the pressure of civilization has most often only restricted the range of our wilderness animals, some of man's structures have resulted in closer relations with other creatures. Our highways and roads take their share of furry casualties each year, but they also provide an excellent viewing post for millions of travellers. As long as the occupants of a car are careful and aware of the dangers of too close an approach, the opportunity to view mammals from a car can be rewarding.

Many mammals use the highway as a relief from the close quarters of the bush. When they emerge on the road, however, they are often confused by the speed and bright lights of the traffic. The disadvantages that man suffers in the bush because of his poor sense of smell and hearing are thus equalized. An animal on the road is also exposed to predators, those which attack their prey in the open, and those scavengers which find road-kills to be a ready source of food.

The type of rapport that can be established in this way is, of course, limited, but it is a step in the direction of a more genuine understanding of our place in the ecology of this continent. Only through such understanding will man be able to preserve our wilderness for future generations.

117

PART FIVE
VANISHING SPECIES

The black-footed ferret is not your typical lovable Disneyland kind of animal. Small, stealthy and quick, with cold little eyes peering from a black face mask, it prowls by night and preys on sleeping prairie dogs in their burrows. When told that the ferret is nearly extinct, few of us summon up more than a yawn.

Yet the ferret belongs on earth as much as any of us. It was once a plentiful and proper part of nature's balance, and we should grieve its passing. Unseen in Canada for years, barely clinging to life in the United States, it is another item in the dreary catalogue of man's destruction of the natural world.

The ferret's case is doubly shameful, for we have destroyed this creature incidentally, while ravaging *another* species. A century ago this particular member of the weasel family lived all across the North American prairie. Billions of prairie dogs also inhabited the grassland in acres of underground 'towns.'

The black-footed ferret is one of the rarest mammals in the Western Hemisphere. An aggressive animal, the ferret is chiefly nocturnal.

The ferrets haunted the burrows, killing and eating the chubby rodents. (Prairie dogs resemble the familiar prairie 'gopher' but the latter, technically, is a form of ground squirrel.)

Nevertheless, prairie dogs flourished until the west was settled. Then they continued to eat grass as before (except now it was known as 'pasture') and they also devoured grain crops (which to the prairie dog must have seemed like some kind of fantastic welfare grant). Sometimes a rancher's horse or a farmer's cow broke a leg in a prairie dog hole. All of this was too much for the settlers who brooked no interference in their rape of the land. Their instinctive reaction to any 'pest' was: obliterate it.

They almost succeeded in this case, in a long-running campaign with poison and gas. Only three prairie dog colonies remain in Canada now, and only one, in southern Saskatchewan, is protected—by the Saskatchewan Natural History Society.

As the prairie dogs diminished so did the ferrets. Poison got many of them; the rest simply lost their food and shelter when the prairie dogs were killed and the burrows ploughed under. Since 1955 only about fifty-five ferrets have been sighted, virtually all in the Dakotas and some merely as roadside corpses. Wind Cave National Park in South Dakota has a protected prairie dog town where both species might be coaxed back from the brink of extinction. So far, though, the chances seem slim. In 1972 two males and four females were live-trapped and taken to the Patuxent Wildlife Research Centre in Maryland, where naturalists hoped to breed them and gradually replenish the wild population. Unfortunately, all the females died of distemper.

And so the black-footed ferret is frequently cited as the rarest mammal in North America. But it is only one of hundreds in danger around the world. The authoritative *Red Data Book*, published by the International Union for Conservation of Nature and Natural Resources, catalogues some 271 species or subspecies in danger of extinction. Even this list is incomplete. The World Wildlife Fund, a charitable organization associated with the IUCN, suggests that as many as 900 kinds of mammals may be in danger.

The *Red Data Book* fails, for example, to mention most of Canada's endangered mammals. Dr N. S. Novakowski, of the Canadian Wildlife Service in Ottawa, cites a dozen endangered species or subspecies once common to this country – from Vancouver Island's Roosevelt elk to Newfoundland's pine marten – plus forty-four others peripheral to Canada, including moles, mice, foxes, bats, skunks, and squirrels. His list, in turn, does not include the polar bear or various whales that are the object of some concern.

Endangered lists will never be wholly accurate. For one thing, numbers become obsolete almost before they can get into print. Also, naturalists disagree on exactly when a creature *is* endangered. There is no precise rule; each case is slightly different. One obvious warning signal, however, is when losses persistently exceed the rate of replenishment. This can be significant even with large populations. As in the case of the plains bison, a vast number can be annihilated in a few years.

At the turn of the century, prairie dog towns covering hundreds of miles and containing millions of individuals were reported. The threat that these towns posed to livestock hastened their demise.

120

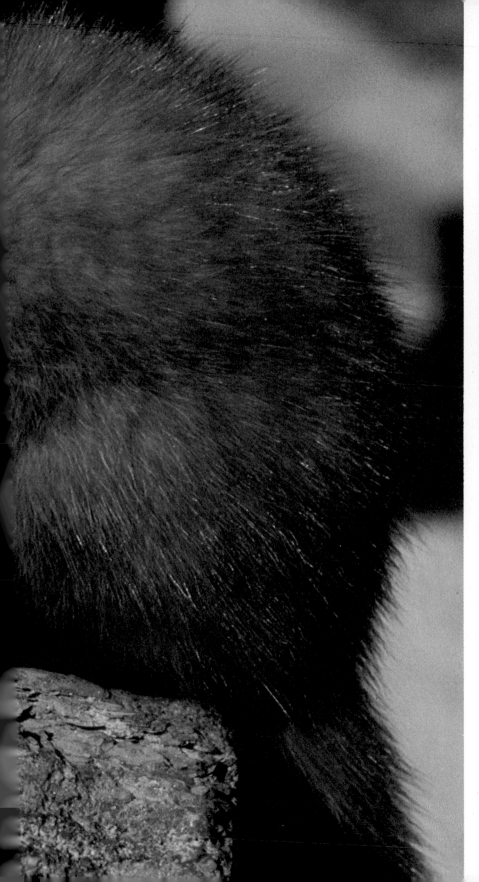

Newfoundland's rarities

The Arctic hare (above) and the pine marten (left) were both once abundant in Newfoundland.

The pine marten was subjected to heavy trapping and is now restricted to isolated areas on the island. Martens often fall victim to traps set for other members of the weasel family and squirrels. As with the ferret, the marten has often been the unintended victim of man's effort to trap other animals.

The Arctic hare was also a victim of man's ignorance. The varying hare was introduced into Newfoundland in 1864 and again in 1900. It soon became a serious competitor of the Arctic hare. The moose, introduced in 1904, further depleted food supplies.

As logging expands the regions of cleared land, the Arctic hare finds more and more habitat that is to its liking. It may be that the destruction of Newfoundland's forests will allow the Arctic hare to expand again in both numbers and range.

123

Even if the numbers are stable, a small population in a limited habitat may be in peril, particularly on an island. One such island is Madagascar in the Indian Ocean off Africa's mainland. It is one of the world's most remarkable natural 'museums.' Twenty-four of its rare mammals are on the official endangered list, including several species of lemur.

---

22   THREAT TO SURVIVAL

The rarest and strangest of these is the aye-aye, a scrawny tree-dwelling primate, not much bigger than a squirrel, with squeaky voice, eyes like shiny shoe-buttons and an extraordinarily long middle finger that digs grubs and larvae out of tree bark. Its habitat is steadily dwindling as developers cut into the forests. At the same time, many Malagasy people shoot the aye-aye on sight, convinced that it is an evil sorcerer. Today only about fifty aye-ayes remain on Madagascar – and on earth.

Rare as it is, the aye-aye shares one thing with every mammal in the world: the greatest threat to its survival is man.

Ultimate extinction is every creature's fate, of course; *Homo sapiens* will be no exception. Species live a few million years at most. Some then vanish entirely, through their inability to change. More often, though, they evolve into other forms. The horse, which has made such a profound contribution to human history, began fifty million years ago as a little animal about a foot high, with four toes on each rear foot and three on each front foot.

There's a vast difference between that natural process and today's methodical destruction. Of the 120 species and subspecies of mammals known to have vanished since 1600 (when scientific records became reasonably accurate), about 75 per cent were destroyed by man. Worse yet, the rate is accelerat-

The wood bison, a very rare species, is a relative of the plains bison. When rediscovered recently, the total wood bison population was about 200, but with protection, it has been increasing.

125

ing: about seventy of those mammals became extinct in the last hundred years.

Most of them succumbed either to man-made changes to their environment or to direct slaughter. By 1935, for instance, persistent hunting wiped out the Queen Charlotte Island caribou of British Columbia. In the same decade, hunting, trapping and poisoning finished off the great plains wolf (once commonly known as the buffalo wolf because it roamed with herds of bison) and the Newfoundland wolf.

Heavy trapping nearly exterminated the pine marten of Newfoundland; the few survivors are now protected. Hunting is threatening several species of bear, such as the Lillooet grizzly and Chelan grizzly of British Columbia. The Roosevelt elk has been eliminated from the B.C. mainland; only a handful survive on Vancouver Island.

The endangered eastern cougar, or panther, is so secretive – and so invariably fired upon by gunslingers when it *is* sighted – that most eastern Canadians think it is extinct. A prominent naturalist and authority on the panther, Bruce S. Wright of New Brunswick, has estimated that twenty-five to fifty remain in his own province and perhaps only one hundred still survive in all of eastern North America down to Florida (where the animal is protected).

We now know that the panther is not a menace; that the predator has its rightful place in nature's scheme of things. Its inroads on livestock are negligible. Bruce Wright has cited dozens of cases where the panther has run away from humans. But the primitive blood-lust and hatred of 'wild cats' lurks in hunters, farmers, ranchers, and small boys of all ages. No province from Saskatchewan east protects any species of cougar, even with so much as a limited hunting season. Cougars, east and west, badly need sanctuary.

The Arctic hare of Newfoundland is the near-victim of another kind of interference. In 1864 and 1900 men introduced a second species of hare to the island. It reproduced rapidly and competed for food. Moose were brought in, further depleting the food supply. Now, through a quirk in man's onslaught on nature, the Arctic hare may be getting a second chance. The logging industry, in cutting down Newfoundland's forests, is inadvertently clearing new habitats for the little animal.

The northern kit fox is a victim of both direct and indirect human predation. A century ago it ranged over most of the prairie provinces and the Dakotas. Not much bigger than a cat, guileless and trusting by nature, the yellow-brown fox dined on mice, gophers, rabbits, birds, lizards, and large insects. Now and then, though, it took a barnyard chicken, which was enough to send settlers running for their guns.

What with the shooting, trapping, and snaring, the ploughing up of prairie, and the poison set out for coyotes and wolves, the kit fox was scarce by the turn of the century. By the 1920s it had almost vanished. A Saskatchewan naturalist, who described the animal's call as 'soft and plaintive, somewhat suggestive of the mourning dove,' last heard it in 1964, in the vicinity of some abandoned coal mines. Survivors exist in the United States and could be transplanted here, *if* we give the kit fox sanctuary. In 1973 a ranching family near Calgary was planning to do exactly that, on their own property.

Sanctuary has been the salvation of many endangered animals. It saved the rare wood bison, for one. A few decades ago only about 300 members of this cousin of the plains buffalo survived in the Northwest Territories south of Great Slave Lake. Later the species seemed to have disappeared through interbreeding with plains buffalo in Wainwright National Park. Then in 1957 the Canadian Wildlife Service discovered 200 wood bison in an isolated corner of the park. Medical care saved the herd from TB and anthrax; further isolation in the big wilderness park has kept the species pure.

---

23 INDISCRIMINATE SLAUGHTER

Parks may be the last hope, too, for the Rocky Mountain bighorn and the California bighorn. Each winter these wild sheep come down from the high country for winter forage.

The northern kit fox is probably extinct in Canada in its wild form. This photograph was taken at the Alberta Game Farm.

Too often, except in parks, they find their traditional grazing land stripped by range cattle. Without winter feed, they perish.

Protection in parks and sanctuaries is surely the last chance also for the Vancouver Island wolf. It is nearly extinct, driven back by hunting and development into remote corners of the island. Indeed, wolves everywhere continue to be relentlessly persecuted. A random example: for three years the North American Association for Preservation of Predatory Animals took two pet wolves, Clem and Jethro, on tours of the continent, in an educational campaign for children. Then one day in 1973, a New York City woman broke into their trailer and deliberately fed them chicken necks laced with lethal doses of strychnine.

Until the early 1970s, Ontario allowed wolf hunting from aircraft and paid a bounty on wolves. Even now some municipalities maintain the bounty, an act that the Federation of Ontario Naturalists condemns. In most provinces any number of wolves can be killed on private land, year round. The pioneer belief that wolves are a natural enemy of man still prevails, although it was never entirely true.

All of this is a pity, maintains Bob Ingraham of the Canadian Wildlife Federation, because people might actually learn something about peacemaking from the wolf. A quarrel among them rarely ends in death or serious injury, he claims. Instead, the subordinated wolf will expose his belly to attack, whereupon the dominant wolf will slink away, having established his superiority.

In some parts of Canada wolves and coyotes are hunted from snowmobiles. Apart from being illegal this is thoroughly unsporting. Regulated hunting has its function, whether or not it is to one's personal taste. It is a form of game management. Its fees help pay for the protection of wildlife in closed season. But the high-powered rifle with telescopic sight, and other modern hunting accessories, including the infamous snowmobile, have pretty well taken the last semblance of contest from this so-called sport.

The timber or gray wolf is hunted mercilessly from the ground and the air, and extinction may be near in some areas.

129

Similarly, a polar bear hunted from aircraft or power boats has no chance. Both tactics have been used in international waters, beyond the three-mile limit, and conservationists hope to put an end to it. Alaska, in the meantime, has banned polar bear hunting. In the Northwest Territories it is still permitted on a quota basis, as part of the traditional right of the native people. This in turn has introduced a new form of northern enterprise: some Eskimos now let white men bag the community quota of bear, in return for handsome cash payments. This is presumably easier and more profitable than carving soapstone.

Hunting as a contribution to the welfare of native people, even in this dubious manner, can perhaps be tolerated a little longer, if the animal population is carefully monitored. But the reasons for and methods of killing in certain other jurisdictions are a throwback to the dark ages.

In East Africa, according to the author Joy Adamson, leopards and cheetahs are killed by forcing a red-hot metal bar into the rectum. That way, there's no damage to the pelt. Both species are headed for extinction and hunting them by any method is illegal. But bootleg leopard and cheetah skins bring $1,000 each in Africa, and there, as elsewhere, laws and law enforcement are too weak to deter poachers at those kinds of stakes. The only hope for these animals, as for the North American alligator, is a ban on the use of skins.

---

24 INTERNATIONAL CONSCIENCE

Some of the 'trophies' resulting from the hunt would be laughable, if it weren't so hard on the animal population. In East Africa the tails of gnus are sold as souvenir fly-swatters, and hollowed-out elephant feet are exported as waste paper baskets. The Indian rhinoceros was almost a goner until chemists recently established that powdered rhinoceros horn is *not* an aphrodisiac.

Mammals are not entirely without help or hope in their struggle for survival. In Canada the federal Wildlife Service, various provincial agencies, numerous associations of natu-ralists, and a growing number of concerned individuals are devoted to the task.

Around the world, the IUCN keeps tabs on the danger levels of species while the World Wildlife Fund has been largely responsible for the survival of such mammals as the aye-aye, the Javan rhinoceros, and the Bengal tiger. In 1971 the Fund launched a world-wide appeal for one million dollars to save other creatures.

Another international effort may also save some animal lives. In 1973 delegates from eighty nations, including Canada, met in Washington to draft a treaty regulating trade in endangered species: a kind of Magna Carta for wild creatures. For example, the 178 species or subspecies of mammals rated in danger of extinction at that time were covered by regulations that practically ban all trade, except perhaps for propagation in captivity. A second list of seventy-eight mammals to be 'carefully watched' includes the polar bear, grey wolf, all North American brown and grizzly bears, and the Rocky Mountain bighorn.

Publishing such lists has its drawbacks. Many conferees feared that poachers and speculators would rush to stockpile pelts and skins before the treaty was ratified. 'We have provided a comprehensive shopping list for those who trade in rare or endangered species,' said one delegate.

Others worried that as one species was protected the hunting pressure would shift to others. 'It became apparent that no animal can be safe from exploitation for long,' reported *Audubon* magazine. Accordingly, the convention made provision for speedy additions to the list, as necessary.

On the matter of whaling, though, the delegates seemed to knuckle under to the International Whaling Commission, a regulatory body that has done a mediocre job of protecting those badly abused mammals. The Washington convention included on its endangered list only those whales – the bowhead, blue, right, humpback, and grey – that the IWC placed

This bighorn sheep family is seen in its natural habitat in Alberta, with Mount Rundle in the background. The winter food supply of these mountain dwellers is threatened by ranging cattle.

130

Polar bear at bay

While the wild animals of Canada were hunted for centuries by the native population, serious depletion did not occur. Eskimos are still allowed to hunt the polar bear, and although they now have rifles to replace their spears, they do not threaten the polar bear with extinction.

Here an Eskimo from the village of Grise Fiord, on Ellesmere Island, follows his dogs as they pursue a polar bear across the ice of Jones Sound. The dogs first harry the bear, dashing in when he turns on them; then they slow the bear down or hold him at bay, while the hunter catches up.

Even after he is wounded (above), *the bear remains standing, although he is still surrounded by dogs. After the hunter has shot the bear, he will tie his dogs' traces to the carcass and return with it to his sled.*

This method of hunting is virtually unchanged from the primitive methods. Only the addition of a gun gives the Eskimo an added advantage.

A polar bear hunted from an airplane or power boat has no chance against man. Even with all its magnificent strength, and speed, it is powerless to combat these 'sportsmen.'

under a moratorium in 1965. Additional species will be added only after consultation with the IWC.

No whales are on the secondary list of mammals. Even should they be added, IWC members – including Japan and the Soviet Union, which account for 85 per cent of the world's whale catch – are exempt from the regulations. In practical terms, then, the Washington treaty did nothing for whales.

Yet the whaling industry has one of the most disgraceful records in the long, tacky history of man, the hunter. The right whale, which has several subspecies, has been almost exterminated. The humpback, which once numbered at least 22,000 in Antarctic waters, was down to 3,000 by the late 1960s. The blue whale – largest mammal that ever lived: up to 100 feet long and weighing as much as 120 tons – once numbered around 40,000 in the Antarctic. In 1963 survivors were estimated at about 600; since then whalers have killed more than 700.

Once, about a half million bowheads swam the oceans of the world. The bowhead is a spectacular fifty-ton monster, whose head makes up a third of its body. This species, too, is down to a few hundred.

25 PRESERVING NATURE'S TREASURES

Although the IWC is ostensibly devoted to conservation, other conservationists claim that it is industry dominated and has no real clout. It may have slowed the slaughter since it was founded in 1946, but an outright ten-year ban is a better way to give the whales a chance. This proposal, espoused by Project Jonah, an international movement headed in Canada by author Farley Mowat, is of course violently opposed by commercial whalers. (Canada, to its credit, got out

The range of all grizzlies is now restricted mainly to parks and reserves. These barren ground grizzlies belong to a group that is now generally protected.

135

of commercial whaling in 1973.)

There's a precedent, of sorts, for a total ban on the hunting of a sea creature. It saved the northern sea otter, although mankind deserves little credit, because the ban was levied *after* the animal was believed extinct. A century ago millions of sea otters, which are about three times the size of the fresh water species, swam and frolicked up and down the Pacific coast from the Aleutian Islands to California. Then Russian and American hunters discovered that the pelts were immensely valuable. The slaughter was so methodical and complete that by 1910 not one otter could be found.

Only then did Britain, Russia, the United States and Japan join in a treaty making the hunt illegal.

Decades passed. Then, miraculously, a few otters appeared off California in 1938. By 1969 the numbers were sufficient that thirty from Alaska could be released off the northwestern coast of Vancouver Island. But, reports Dr N. S. Novakowski of the Canadian Wildlife Service, although the transplant seems to have taken hold there is some doubt that the otters are reproducing. There is a new threat to them now: water pollution.

Tough laws, rigidly enforced, are the mammals' best hope, but there are other ways of perpetuating the species. The Arabian oryx, a kind of antelope, and Przewalski's horse, a remnant of the original wild horse, are both thriving in captivity while their future in the wild is almost hopeless. As human population and pressures increase, more such rare creatures may have to be bred and sheltered in zoos, perhaps specially designed for this purpose.

As a new twist on controlled breeding, there is even a sperm bank for animals in San Francisco. It followed the discovery that some creatures – so far, mostly amphibians – can be bred by using frozen sperm. An egg cell is taken from a live female and its nucleus replaced with that from the frozen sperm of a dead animal of similar species. The egg is then re-inserted in the female's body. The offspring is said to be the same as the dead animal – an exact genetic copy of the animal from which the sperm was taken.

As of late 1973 the technique had not been tried on mammals but some enthusiasts see it as a way of saving animals on the verge of extinction. It was even suggested that the sperm of a mammoth recovered from a frozen carcass in the icy bogs of Siberia, might be transplanted to the egg of an elephant, and so bring a mammoth back to life on earth.

To the true naturalist, breeding in captivity – even by so esoteric a method as the sperm bank – is a poor second-best to natural life in a natural habitat. But where? Cities, resorts, airports, and industrial sites are marching inexorably over country and forest. Unless we make a more concerted attempt to salvage our remaining wilderness, there will be no place left to hide, for beast *or* man.

In this regard, no effort is too trifling. Private individuals with rural property can help. Ontario's fish and wildlife branch, for one, distributes a booklet that shows how private landowners with modest labour and expense can plant shrubs that attract various birds and arrange ground cover to shelter various small animals.

The major requirement, however, is more parks. In centennial year a senior member of Canada's federal government told a parliamentary committee that we should create forty to sixty new parks by the year 2000 and that the land should be acquired by 1985, before it was lost to development. That meant two or three new parks in each of the subsequent eighteen years. But T. G. Henderson, executive director of the National and Provincial Parks Association of Canada, is 'very pessimistic about the future,' and adds that if 'we don't get all the necessary land by the end of the 1970s we won't get it at all.'

Canada has been woefully slow in other kinds of legislative action. Ontario, in 1971, was the first province to pass an Endangered Species Act – a good beginning, with stiff penalties of as much as $3,000 and/or six months in jail for violators. But as of the end of 1973 the province had named only two birds and two reptiles to its endangered list.

Nationally, the Canada Wildlife Act was passed in mid-1973, with an endangered species clause. It will permit the federal government to enter into cooperative agreements with the provinces to protect wildlife, and will result in a national endangered species list. But the actual list, and the proposed

The early whalers wantonly killed off thousands of marine mammals in their search for oil, whalebone, and ivory.

136

Accidental victims

Many animals are incidental victims of man's civilization. Not only does man hunt, reduce habitat, and threaten the food supply of many species of animals, his way of life also introduces additional hazards with which wild animals must attempt to cope.

Over the past century, the railway has slashed through much of the Canadian wilderness, cutting through the trails and migratory paths of many animals, and posing a constant threat to all. In some areas, animals receive only brief warning of an approaching train, and a pause on the tracks, like that of the doe elk (above), *can be fatal.*

Other animals find that they must contend with the intrusion of man's garbage into the wilderness. The porcupine (left) *had become trapped in a tin can, probably while attempting to reach food at the bottom of it. The photographer found this porcupine in the woods near Dorcas Bay, Ontario. In order to extricate the trapped animal, he had to twist the can with a circular movement to free the quills from the inturned edge of the can. A very tricky manoeuvre! The animal was quite groggy when released and may have been trapped for some time. It would no doubt have died had it not been discovered and rescued.*

139

plants and dogs and cats and budgerigars. . . . I believe he should take just as great pains to look after the natural treasures which inspire him as he does to preserve his man-made treasures in art galleries and museums.'

The creatures of nature *are* rare treasures. The wondrous chemistry of evolution made them exactly what they are. A wood bison may smell no different than a plains bison, and neither may smell very good. A black-footed ferret may look, to most of us, like any other weasel. But each *is* different. If they vanish, we will never see their like on earth again.

And if we let this happen, knowingly, because of a wanton shot or a careless dab of poison, it will be a particularly wicked form of murder, and an even worse form of arrogance. We have not yet earned the status of gods-on-earth.

ROBERT COLLINS

Moose are hunted for trophies and for meat. This familiar sight can be seen along many of Canada's highways during the moose-hunting season.

142

Zoos and sanctuaries

Along with nearly everything else in our modern world, our contemporary conception of the zoo is changing. Progressive thinkers and planners now see the theory, structure, and function of the zoo in ecological terms. No longer is the zoo seen as a place where animals are caged simply for the entertainment and education of masses of people. Modern zoos continue to entertain and educate, but in addition they act as centres of scientific investigation, as safe and comfortable homes for scores of different species, and as sanctuaries where endangered species can survive, breed, and increase their numbers.

In the past, 'menagerie' type zoos were stocked from nature. Expeditions captured rare animals and delivered them into captivity, where they lived in cages and pits, often succumbing to premature death through improper care. The environment of a menagerie also contributed greatly to the death rate. Like men in prisons, deprived of the natural activities of their species, many animals became despondent. This was particularly true of the larger mammals, which require great areas of open space in order to move about and sense the freedom all animals require to be healthy and happy.

Today, virtually all specimens that a zoo acquires come from other zoos. Strict laws forbid the exportation of native animals from many countries. But more important, most species are now represented in the world's zoo population. Where animals are breeding and increasing their numbers, it is possible for the various zoos to trade with one another, thus increasing the variety of their species.

When we think of the endangered species, we tend to think of countries on the other side of the world. The Indian tiger, for example, has declined over the last half-century from some 40,000 animals to less than 2,000. In Africa, the rhinoceros faces extinction, and in the oceans certain species of whale may soon be hunted out of existence. But actually, all animals face severe dangers as the galloping human population fills the earth. In Canada, the wood bison once numbered in the thou-

---

This camel, looking almost as much at home in the snow as it would on sand, resides at the Okanagan Game Farm in Penticton, British Columbia.

sands, particularly in northern Alberta and the southeast Mackenzie District of the Northwest Territories. Due to hunting, climatic conditions, and hybridization over the last hundred years, this creature was thought to be extinct. However, a small group in Wood Buffalo Park was identified, isolated, and transported to its historic range, where it is now under protection. A breeding herd to provide further wood bison stock for transplant is now isolated in Elk Island National Park. National parks, wildlife sanctuaries, and zoos all play a part in preserving rare and endangered species, by creating a habitat where they can live in peace.

It has happened in the past, and will no doubt continue to happen, that rare animals bred in zoos can be returned to the wild once their numbers increase.

The ability to breed in captivity may be essential to the survival of some species, like big horn sheep (above). The buffalo and its calf (right) are kept in the buffalo paddock at Banff National Park.

A game farm is basically a large area set aside where a number of animals can live without the constant interference of human spectators, and without the presence of cages, moats, and fences. The great value of a game farm is that the animals can pursue a natural life style, live out normal lifespans, and reproduce freely. For this reason, game farms are excellent places for scientists to study the animals of foreign lands under the most natural conditions. This arrangement is obviously best for the animals as well; and their physical condition, energy and playfulness show that they are happier without the restrictions of the menagerie.

The ideal modern zoo would combine most of the advantages of the game farm with the traditional accessibility of the animals to the public. Scientific observation of the animals in a natural habitat would also be combined with the intense care and observation of the traditional zoo. This can be accomplished by designing the zoo very carefully so that animals live in a natural environment, while their human observers remain as unobtrusive as possible. Large areas can be set up where compatible animals can live naturally together, their man-made shelters camouflaged in the underbrush, and their human audience kept at a respectful distance.

The traditional cages of menagerie zoos, and the crowding they mean to the animals, are a major cause of boredom, which animals feel as acutely as human beings. Only a large amount of space, and a natural environment, can alleviate this problem. From a lion's point of view, imagine the difference between life in a cage that is perhaps ten times as big as it is, and life with a dozen or more other lions in a few acres of land that resembles its native Africa, with even the plants specially imported to reproduce its natural home. Here the lions can mate, raise their young, and enjoy a comfortable old age, while millions of human beings are amazed and enlightened by being close to a real pride of lions. The difference lies in the viewpoint; rather than human convenience we must consider what life is like for

the animals we hold captive in our zoos. When we go to the trouble of creating a natural setting for the lions to live in, we get the bonus of being able to observe them as they are in the wild.

The Metropolitan Toronto Zoo is the only zoo in the world which uses a geographical approach to providing a natural setting for its inhabitants. This seven-hundred-acre site is divided along geographical lines, with the animals from the same part of the world sharing the same section of the zoo. This plan provides a lesson in geography for the visitors to this zoo. More importantly, however, it allows the zoo's designers to reproduce the terrain of a part of the world, so that the 5,000 animals will all live in their natural surroundings. Compatible animals share the same open area, and predators are kept separate by moats and fences which are largely invisible to the visitor. The animals themselves decide if the Canadian weather is too severe for them, and go into their heated and camouflaged shelters whenever they wish. The animals carry on their lives, rearing their young, and enjoying their safety, largely as if they were not being observed.

Above all, the Toronto Zoo is a breeding zoo. Here success is acknowledged only when the animals feel comfortable enough to breed, when the young are accepted and reared naturally, and when second generations themselves reproduce. Only when the species-preserving activities are all carried out normally, and the animals are able to live essentially as they would in the wild, can the function of the zoo be called successful. Although an abandoned or orphaned baby zoo animal will always be hand-reared by human attendants, every effort is made to ensure that mother and baby are not separated. There is no thought of separating the young to stock a children's zoo, even though this practice has been both widespread and popular in the past.

As our world shrinks, and we become more aware of our environment and our relationship with it, our traditional fascination with animals, particularly from far-off places, will probably grow. Along with that interest we must develop an appreciation for the wisdom of nature, and respect the natural condition of the animals we shelter and study in our zoos. If we do this, zoos will continue to be a source of wonder, amusement, and knowledge. And they will serve a further purpose in re-establishing the balance of nature on the earth.

The most popular attraction at the Vancouver Aquarium is the whale display. Skana, the most famous of these whales, was captured in Puget Sound in 1967.

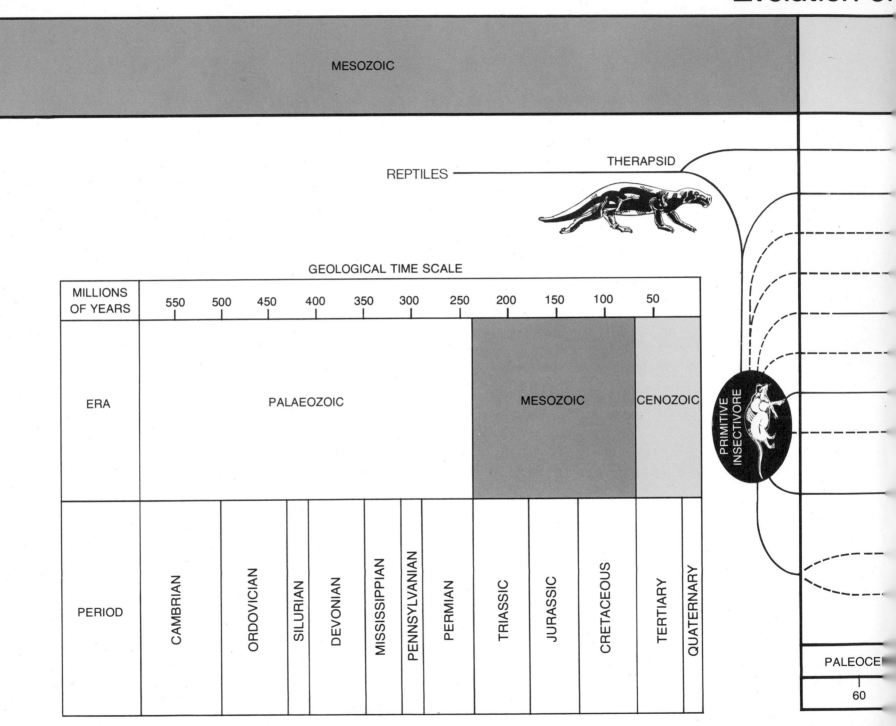

MESOZOIC

REPTILES ——————————————— THERAPSID

GEOLOGICAL TIME SCALE

MILLIONS OF YEARS	550	500	450	400	350	300	250	200	150	100	50

ERA	PALAEOZOIC	MESOZOIC	CENOZOIC

PERIOD	CAMBRIAN	ORDOVICIAN	SILURIAN	DEVONIAN	MISSISSIPPIAN	PENNSYLVANIAN	PERMIAN	TRIASSIC	JURASSIC	CRETACEOUS	TERTIARY	QUATERNARY

PRIMITIVE INSECTIVORE

PALEOCE

60

150

Canadian Mammals

CENOZOIC				
			MONOTREME	
			MARSUPIAL	
			LAGOMORPHA	
			RODENTIA	
			PRIMATE	
			CHIROPTERA	
			INSECTIVORA	
			CETACEA	
			PINNIPEDIA	
			CARNIVORA	
			ARTIODACTYLA	
			PERISSODACTYLA	
EOCENE	OLIGOCENE	MIOCENE		PLEIST-OCENE
50 40	30	20 10		

MILLIONS OF YEARS

MAMMALS FOUND IN CANADA

151

BIBLIOGRAPHY

ALLEN, GLOVER M., 'Extinct and Vanishing Mammals of the Western Hemisphere,' American Committee for International Wildlife Protection, Special Publication No, 11, 1942

ANDERSON, R.M., *Catalogue of Canadian Recent Mammals*, Ottawa: National Museum of Canada, Bulletin No. 102, 1946

BURT, WILLIAM H. and RICHARD P. GROSSENHEIDER, *A Field Guide to the Mammals*, Boston: Houghton Mifflin Co., 1952

BURT, WILLIAM H., *The Mammals of Michigan*, Ann Arbor: University of Michigan Press, 1946

BURT, WILLIAM H., *Mammals of the Great Lakes Region*, Ann Arbor: University of Michigan Press, 1957

CAMERON, AUSTIN W., *Canadian Mammals*, Ottawa: National Museum of Canada, (revised) 1964

CANADIAN WILDLIFE FEDERATION, *Endangered Wildlife in Canada*, Ottawa: CWF, 1970

CARAS, ROGER A., *Last Chance on Earth*, Philadelphia: Chilton Book Co., 1966

CARAS, ROGER A., *North American Mammals*, New York: Meredith Corp., 1967

CARRINGTON, RICHARD and THE EDITORS OF LIFE, *The Mammals*, New York: Time Inc., 1963

COWAN, IAN MCTAGGART and CHARLES J. GUIGUET, *The Mammals of British Columbia*, Victoria: Provincial Museum, Handbook, No. 11, 1960

FISHER, JAMES, *Zoos of the World*, Garden City: Natural History Press, 1967

FITTER, RICHARD S.R., *Vanishing Wild Animals of the World*, London: Midland Bank in conjunction with Kaye & Ward, 1968

GUNDERSON, HARVEY L. and JAMES R. BEER, *The Mammals of Minnesota*, Minneapolis: University of Minnesota Press, 1953

HALSTEAD, L.B., *The Pattern of Evolution*, Edinburgh: Oliver and Boyd, 1969

HASS, HANS, *Mammals of the World*, London: Methuen Publishing, 1956

HOTTON III, NICHOLAS, *The Evidence of Evolution*, Washington: American Heritage Publishing Co., 1968

INTERNATIONAL UNION FOR CONSERVATION OF NATURE AND NATURAL RESOURCES, *Red Data Book*, Morges: 1966

LAWRENCE, R.D., *Wildlife in Canada*, Toronto: Thomas Nelson & Sons (Canada) Ltd., 1970

LE GROS CLARK, W.E., *The Antecedents of Man*, Chicago: Quadrangle Books Inc., 1959

LEOPOLD, ALDO, *A Sand County Almanac*, London: Oxford University Press, 1949

MATTHIESSEN, PETER, *Wildlife in America*, New York: Viking Press Inc., 1959

MOORE, RUTH and THE EDITORS OF LIFE, *Evolution*, New York: Time Inc., 1962

MORRIS, DESMOND, *The Mammals*, London: Hodder & Stoughton, 1965

NOBILE, P., and J. DEEDY, (eds.), *The Complete Ecology Fact Book*, New York: Doubleday & Company, Inc., 1972

NOVAKOWSKI, N.S., 'Endangered Canadian Mammals,' Ottawa: *Canadian Field Naturalist*, Volume 84, 1970

PETERSON, RANDOLPH L., *The Mammals of Eastern Canada*, Toronto: Oxford University Press, 1966

PINNEY, ROY, *Vanishing Wildlife*, New York: Dodd Mead & Co., 1963

ROMER, ALFRED S., *The Vertebrate Story*, Chicago: University of Chicago Press, 4th Edition, 1959

RUSSELL, L.S., *The Mastodon*, Toronto: University of Toronto Press/Royal Ontario Museum, 1964

SANDERSON, IVAN, *Living Mammals of the World*, New York: Doubleday & Company, Inc., 1955

SETON, ERNEST THOMPSON, *The Lives of Game Animals* (4 volumes), New York: Schocken Books, Inc., 1953

SIMON, NOEL M. and PAUL GEROUDET, *Last Survivors*, New York: World Publishing Co., 1970

STORER and USINGER, *General Zoology*, New York: McGraw-Hill Inc., 4th Edition, 1971

URQUHART, F.A., *Changes in the Fauna of Ontario*, Toronto: University of Toronto Press, 1957

WOOD, F. and D., *Animals in Danger*, New York: Dodd Mead & Co., 1968

WRIGHT, BRUCE S., *The Eastern Panther*, Toronto: Clarke Irwin & Co. Ltd., 1972

WYNNE-EDWARDS, V.C., *Animal Dispersion in Relation to Social Behaviour*, New York: Hafner Publishing Co. Inc., 1962

YAPPLER, L. and G., *The World After the Dinosaurs*, Garden City: National History Press, 1970

YOUNG, J.Z., *The Life of Mammals*, London: Oxford University Press, 1957

ZISWILER, V., *Extinct and Vanishing Animals*, New York: Springer-Verlag New York, Inc., 1967

INDEX

ACKNOWLEDGEMENTS AND CREDITS

The authors and editors of this volume wish to thank the following organizations and individuals whose assistance with the text and illustrations made this book possible: Fred Breummer, Montreal; Bill Brooks, Toronto; Canadian Wildlife Services, Ottawa; Dr C. S. Churcher, Department of Zoology, University of Toronto; Victor Crich, Toronto; Dr A. Gordon Edmund, Department of Vertebrate Palaeontology, Royal Ontario Museum, Toronto; Dr Donald R. Gunn, Oakville; T. G. Henderson, National Provincial Parks Association, Toronto; Dr W. Irving, Department of Anthropology, University of Toronto; Wayne McLaren, Toronto; Metro Toronto Central Library; N. S. Novakowski, Canadian Wildlife Services, Ottawa; David Payne, Oshawa; Dr R. L. Peterson, Department of Mammalogy, Royal Ontario Museum, Toronto; Marion Price, Library, Royal Ontario Museum, Toronto; Dr Howard Savage, Research Associate, Royal Ontario Museum, Toronto; W. D. Wood, Upper Canada College, Toronto.

Where more than one picture appears on a page, the order of credits is left to right, horizontal separated by commas, vertical separated by semi-colons.

Cover	Cy Hampson
Back Cover	John De Visser
1	Mildred McPhee
2,3	John De Visser
4,5	V. Claerhout
6	Terry Shortt
9	Bill Brooks
10	T. W. Hall
13	Huntley Brown
14,15	Mildred McPhee, Edgar T. Jones, Victor Crich; Norman R. Lightfoot, James M. Richards, Norman R. Lightfoot; Edgar T. Jones, Alma H. Carmichael, Barry Ranford
17,18,19	Huntley Brown
20	T. W. Hall
21	T. W. Hall
22	Valerie J. May

24,25	T. W. Hall, T. W. Hall		97	Cy Hampson
26,27	Huntley Brown		98,99	T. W. Hall
28,29	T. W. Hall		100,101	T. W. Hall
30,31	Susan Gabe		102,103	E. Kuyt
32	Huntley Brown		104,105	Bill Brooks
33	Cy Hampson		106,107	Ted Maginn
35	T. W. Hall		108,109	Valerie J. May, Valerie J. May
36	G. McLean		111	T. W. Hall
38	Bill Brooks		112	John De Visser
40,41	T. W. Hall		114,115	Victor Crich
42,43	Huntley Brown		116,117	David Taylor, T. W. Hall
44	Dr Donald R. Gunn		118	T. W. Hall
46,47	Huntley Brown		120,121	Norman R. Lightfoot
49,50	Huntley Brown		122,123	T. W. Hall, Cy Hampson
52	Huntley Brown		124,125	David Taylor
53	Bill Brooks		127	Robert R. Taylor
54	Cy Hampson		128,129	David Taylor
56	Courtesy of Ministry of Natural Resources, Ontario		131	John De Visser
			132,133	Fred Breummer
58,59	T. W. Hall, T. W. Hall, Horst Ehricht, T. W. Hall		134,135	David Taylor
			137	Courtesy of Fine Art Reference Picture Collection, Metropolitan Toronto Central Library
61	Norman R. Lightfoot		138,139	Victor Crich, T. W. Hall
62	Edgar T. Jones		140,141	Victor Crich
64,65	John Foster		143	T. W. Hall
66,67	Tom Willock		144,145	T. W. Hall
68	Bill Brooks, Cy Hampson		146,147	Valerie J. May
69	T. W. Hall, T. W. Hall		148	Mildred McPhee
70,71	Huntley Brown			
72,73	T. W. Hall			
74,75	Victor Crich, T. W. Hall			
76	T. W. Hall			
78,79	T. W. Hall			
80	T. W. Hall			
82,83	John De Visser, John De Visser			
84,85	Edgar T. Jones			
86	Victor Crich			
88,89	Norman R. Lightfoot			
90,91	Dr Donald R. Gunn			
92,93	Mildred McPhee			
94,95	John De Visser, Alma H. Carmichael			
96	Norman R. Lightfoot			

This book was produced entirely in Canada by: Mono Lino Typesetting Co. Limited/ *Typesetting;* Herzig Somerville Limited/*Film Separation;* Ashton-Potter Limited/ *Printing;* T.H. Best Printing Co. Limited/*Binding. Typefaces: Times New Roman and Helvetica. Paper: 64 lb. Georgian Offset Smooth.*

Printed in Canada